Maps for Family and
Local History

Maps for Family and Local History

The records of the Tithe, Valuation Office and National Farm Surveys

Second revised edition

Geraldine Beech and Rose Mitchell

the national archives

Readers' Guide No. 26

First edition published in 1994 by the Public Record Office (1 873162 17 0)
Second edition first published in 2004 by

The National Archives
Kew, Richmond
Surrey, TW9 4DU, UK

www.nationalarchives.gov.uk

The National Archives was formed when the Public Record Office and the Historical Manuscripts Commission combined in April 2003

© Geraldine Beech and Rose Mitchell 2004

The right of Geraldine Beech and Rose Mitchell to be identified as the Authors of this Work has been asserted by them in accordance with the Copyright, Designs and Patents Act 1988

A catalogue record for this book is available from the British Library

ISBN 1 903365 50 3

Front cover illustration: part of the tithe map of Brentford, Middlesex (IR 30/21/7).
Back cover illustration: cockerell cartouche, detail, from MPI 1/230/6 (formerly part of ADM 79/13).

Typeset by Textype, Cambridge, Cambridgeshire
Printed in the UK by Cromwell Press, Trowbridge, Wiltshire

Contents

Preface   vii

Using the National Archives   ix

Family and local history: using maps in the National Archives   1

1   **Introduction to the three surveys**   11

2   **The mid-nineteenth-century Tithe Commission**   13

3   **The Valuation Office survey, 1910–15**   36

4   **The National Farm Survey of England and Wales, 1941–3**   69

5   **How to find an Ordnance Survey sheet number**   87

6   **Case study across the three surveys: Down St Mary, Devon**   93
     Rose Mitchell

7   **Case study across the three surveys: Darlaston, Staffordshire**   101
     Geraldine Beech

Further reading   110

Index   112

Preface

Maps are among the most visually attractive and most frequently consulted categories of public records. From medieval English estate plans to maps for the 1956 Suez campaign, their geographical and thematic range is enormous. Local historians have long used maps to research changing patterns of occupation and land use, urban development, communications, industry and public amenities. Family historians have, generally speaking, discovered the value of maps much more recently.

It was the greatly increased use by family historians of maps among the public records that prompted William Foot to write *Maps for Family History* (PRO 1994). It was his idea to bring together in a single volume information about three of the major series of maps used by family historians: the tithe, Valuation Office and National Farm Survey records. The resultant book was a ground-breaking venture for the Public Record Office: the first attempt to help researchers to find and understand some of the most frequently consulted series of maps and the textual records they were made to accompany. *Maps for Family History* rapidly became one of the PRO's best-selling publications and it has remained one of the most frequently consulted works of reference in the Map and Large Document Reading Room. In the years since 1994, the Public Record Office has become part of the National Archives (TNA), many finding aids have been made available over the internet through PROCAT (the online catalogue), and *Maps for Family History* has long gone out of print.

Public demand for a re-issue of *Maps for Family History* has led to the writing of the present book, a completely revised and expanded edition. While building substantially on William Foot's work, it seeks to show how the tithe, Valuation Office and National Farm surveys can be of use to local as well as family historians – and for research into such topics as public rights of way, hedgerows, property boundaries, agrarian history and population studies. We hope that it will alert new users to the wealth of information about people and places which these records contain, and help more experienced users to exploit these sources to the full. The provenance for all maps and textual records illustrated in this book is the TNA.

Geraldine Beech and Rose Mitchell

Using the National Archives

The National Archives (TNA) was created on 2 April 2003, when the Public Record Office (PRO) and the Historical Manuscripts Commission (HMC) joined together to form a new organization. The National Archives is the national repository for central government records in the United Kingdom.

The main site at Kew holds the surviving records of British central government from the Domesday Book (1086) to the twentieth century. There are millions of records, which occupy more than 175 kilometres of shelving; another two to three kilometres of documents are added at the beginning of each calendar year. Records of military and naval service, legal proceedings, charters, wills, photographs and one of the world's great accumulations of maps and plans are just a sample of the types of document which make the National Archives an invaluable resource for family and local historians.

The Family Records Centre (FRC) in central London is administered jointly by the National Archives and the General Register Office. It provides access to some of the most important sources for family history research in England and Wales, including birth, marriage and death certificates from 1837 onwards and the population census returns from 1841 to 1901.

Contact details

The National Archives
Kew
Richmond
Surrey
TW9 4DU

The Family Records Centre
1 Myddelton Street
London
EC1R 1UW

Website: **www.nationalarchives.gov.uk**
Telephone: 020 8876 3444

Website: **www.familyrecords.gov.uk/frc**
Telephone: 020 8392 5300

Enquiries and advance ordering of documents at Kew (with exact references only):
Telephone: 020 8392 5200
Fax: 020 8392 5286
Email: **enquiry@nationalarchives.gov.uk**

Opening hours

Monday	9 a.m. to 5 p.m.
Tuesday	10 a.m. to 7 p.m.
Wednesday	9 a.m. to 5 p.m.
Thursday	9 a.m. to 7 p.m.
Friday	9 a.m. to 5 p.m.
Saturday	9.30 a.m. to 5 p.m.

The reading rooms are closed on Sundays, public holidays, and for annual stocktaking – usually the first week of December.

Note that the last time for ordering original documents for same-day production is 4 p.m. on Mondays, Wednesdays and Fridays; 4.30 p.m. on Tuesdays and Thursdays; and 2.30 p.m. on Saturdays.

The National Archives at Kew

The National Archives main site is about 10 minutes' walk from Kew Gardens station, which is on the London Underground District Line and the North London Line Silverlink Metro service. A number of bus routes pass nearby. The site is signposted from the South Circular Road (A205); a free car park is available. Facilities include a restaurant, a bookshop, a reference library, and a small museum.

The National Archives may seem a confusing place on your first visit, but staff are knowledgeable, friendly and happy to help. It is always best to bring with you as much relevant information as you can. If you have access to the internet, it would be worth doing some preliminary research on our website before you come: there are leaflets on many of the most popular areas of research, and a searchable online catalogue of the records, as well as much general information about our services.

You do not need to make an appointment to visit, but a reader's ticket is required to gain access to the research areas and to order documents. To obtain a reader's ticket, you will need to bring some means of personal identification, such as a banker's card, passport or full UK driving licence, if you are a British citizen; and a passport or national identity card, if you are not.

To protect the documents, most of which are unique, eating, drinking and smoking are not permitted in the reading rooms. No personal bags may be taken into the reading rooms: free, self-service lockers are available. You may take a laptop computer into the reading rooms as well as graphite (black lead) pencils, a notebook and up to 10 loose sheets of paper; the use of rubbers, pens (including felt-tips), and coloured pencils is not permitted. Mobile phones may not be used. All original records and reference books should be handled with great care.

Identifying and ordering documents

To view a document at the National Archives, either in its original form or on microform, you need first to identify its document reference. TNA (PRO) document references usually consist of three parts: department code, series number and piece number. When they are transferred to the National Archives, the records of a government department are normally assigned a department code reflecting their provenance: for example, records created by the Ministry of Agriculture and Fisheries commence with the department code **MAF**. Each category of records transferred by a department is then assigned a series number: for example, **MAF 1** is the series of Ministry of Agriculture and Fisheries records which contains enclosure awards and maps made following the General Enclosure Act 1845. Each separate document (known as a 'piece') within a series is given its own individual piece number: for example, the reference for the piece that contains the enclosure award maps of Taunton Deane manor in Somerset is **MAF 1/52**. This is the full reference you need to order the document.

To place an order for an original document, you need a reader's ticket, and a full document reference. Document references can be found by using the printed *PRO Guide* and series lists in the reading rooms or through the online catalogue (PROCAT), which can be accessed via our website or through computer terminals in the reading rooms at Kew and in the Census and Wills Reading Room at the Family Records Centre. PROCAT can be searched using keywords such as a person's name or a place-name. More specific searches can be carried out by specifying dates and/or series references. Do bear in mind, however, that the catalogue was not designed to give the full details about individuals which the documents themselves may contain. So, for example, the catalogue entry for **MAF 1/52** does not give the names of the owners of the lands that were enclosed: you will have to look at the actual document to discover these. If a PROCAT search is successful, document references relevant to your research will be listed on screen.

Once you have the necessary reference, original documents may be ordered via a computerized ordering system and are usually delivered within 30 minutes. Documents on microfilm can be accessed on a self-service basis.

Records held elsewhere

Many records of value for family and local history are held in other record offices and libraries. The National Register of Archives, which is maintained by the National Archives and is available on our website, contains information about the whereabouts of records in local record offices, local studies libraries and other repositories in England and Wales.

Central government records relating to Scotland are held at:

The National Archives of Scotland
HM General Register House
Edinburgh
EH1 3YY

Website: **www.nas.gov.uk**
Telephone: 0131 535 1334

Records relating to Wales are held at:

The National Library of Wales
Aberystwyth
Ceredigion
SY23 3BU

Website: **www.llgc.org.uk**
Telephone: 01970 632800

Family and local history:
using maps in the National Archives

The National Archives holds one of the largest and most varied accumulations of maps in the world. From medieval estate plans to late-twentieth century planning maps, from the streets of London to the wastes of the Arctic, their geographical and thematic spread is probably unsurpassed. However, finding the map you want can be difficult and time-consuming. This introduction explains why the maps in the National Archives are not always easy to find, describes the finding aids that are available, and highlights the principal series of value to the family and local historian which are not treated in detail in this book.

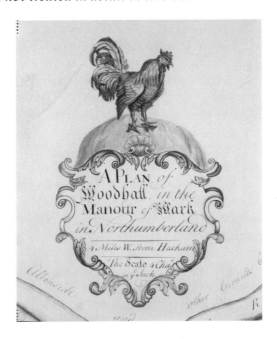

The use of maps by family and local historians has increased enormously in recent decades. Family historians' interests have often extended beyond the simple compilation of a family tree to encompass the daily lives and environment of their ancestors. As a result, many family historians are also local historians, and the interests of the two groups are in many respects similar.

The use of maps varies: some are consulted in an attempt to identify or locate place names which no longer exist; some to increase knowledge of places, buildings and events connected with an individual's life or significant in the history of a locality; some because they are the means of reference to other series of records which are themselves of genealogical or local historical interest.

The National Archives does not have a single, cohesive 'map collection'. Maps are arranged, like other records in the archives, not according to theme, geographical area or publisher, but according to the government department or court of law which created or acquired them. For this reason, certain distinct kinds of map, such as enclosure award maps, estate plans or plans of fortifications, may be distributed among the records of a number of courts or departments. Only a few departments – notably the Foreign Office, the Colonial Office and the War Office – deliberately collected maps: these collections now form discrete record series which are rich sources of printed and manuscript maps. Other departments created maps of a particular kind in the course of their normal activities – the tithe maps, the Valuation Office maps and the National Farm Survey maps, all of which are described in this book, are obvious examples of such maps. Still other departments tended to acquire maps only when they needed geographical information or when a correspondent or informant sent or used a map for information or clarification – illustrating a report to the Admiralty about a voyage of exploration or accompanying papers for a Ministry of Housing and Local Government committee about town planning, for instance. All this makes looking for a map in the National Archives a very different experience from using a map library.

The majority of the maps which are now in the National Archives were transferred together with the letters, reports, registered files or other documents with which they were originally associated in the course of official business. In such cases, there is often no indication in the series list or online catalogue (PROCAT) that a map exists. Although some such maps have been identified and described in the map catalogues and other finding aids (see below), most will be found only by searching. It is known that many thousands of maps remain unidentified and uncatalogued among the records. If you are looking for a particular map which does not appear to be described in the printed catalogues or in the online catalogue, you should first ask yourself which court or department is likely to have made, used or acquired the kind of map you wish to find. A certain amount of lateral thinking may be necessary. Ask yourself which department is likely to have had a particular interest in 'your' area: the Board of Ordnance or the War Office in the case of fortified towns or areas of particular strategic importance; the Admiralty in towns with a strong naval presence (notably Chatham, Plymouth, Portsmouth); the National Coal Board in areas where coal mining was the principal industry; the pre-nationalization railway companies in Swindon, Crewe, Darlington, York and other major railway centres; the Forestry Commission and its predecessors in the New Forest, Forest of Dean and other forested areas; and so on.

Two general leaflets (available at Kew or via the National Archives website) are particularly useful if you are just beginning a search. They are:

- Maps in the National Archives
- Architectural drawings in the National Archives

Many of the most widely used kinds of map are also described in leaflets:

- Admiralty charts
- Common lands
- Enclosure awards and maps
- First World War: military maps
- Foreign, Colonial and Dominions Office maps
- National Farm Survey
- Ordnance Survey
- Public rights of way
- Second World War: military maps
- Tithe records
- Valuation Office records

Traditionally, the Public Record Office map catalogues were organized topographically, since most people looking for a map are interested in a particular geographical area. Four volumes of the catalogue, *Maps and Plans in the Public Record Office*, have been published by the Stationery Office (formerly Her Majesty's Stationery Office):

- *British Isles c. 1410–1860* (published 1967)
- *America and West Indies* (1974)
- *Africa* (1983)
- *Europe and Turkey* (1998)

The Maps, Plans and Drawings Team at the National Archives is now in the course of a long-term project to add the contents of these catalogues and of the supplementary card catalogues to PROCAT.

However, many maps – particularly those in series which consist entirely of maps and plans – are already described, albeit very briefly, in series lists and in PROCAT. Be warned, however: a search in PROCAT for 'Maps AND Jersey', for example, will produce a very different result from a search for 'Map AND Jersey'; and both of these will result in references to maps of New Jersey (USA) and of Jersey in the Channel Islands. To confine your search to maps of Jersey in the Channel Islands, search for 'Maps AND Jersey NOT New' and 'Map AND Jersey NOT New'. Be aware that such a search will probably also produce references to documents *about* maps but which do not necessarily actually *contain* maps.

This book describes three of the series of maps (and the textual records to which they relate) most frequently consulted for family and local history: the mid-nineteenth-century tithe maps, the Valuation Office maps from just before the First World War, and the National Farm Survey from the Second World War. The following are some other series of maps of particular value to the family or local historian.

Enclosure award maps

The enclosure movement of the eighteenth and early nineteenth centuries resulted in extensive redistribution of land. The enclosure award (the formal document which set out the terms of the enclosure) was usually, though not always, accompanied by a map setting out the new allotments of land which would result from the enclosure. Each plot of land on the map was identified by a number which can be related to the accompanying schedule: this usually gives, for each plot of land, the landowner's name, extent of holdings and nature of tenure (freehold, copyhold, etc.); there may also be information about who was to be responsible for maintaining fences, hedges or other boundaries, and about rights of way.

Because enclosure did not take place everywhere, because the pattern of enclosure varied from place to place, and because the legislation under which enclosure was effected differed from time to time, enclosure awards are widely scattered. At the National Archives alone, they may be found among the records of the Court of Common Pleas, the Court of Chancery, the Palatinates of Chester and of Durham, the Duchy of Lancaster, the Land Revenue Record Office and the Ministry of Agriculture. Many enclosure records are held in local record offices: for guides to the location of enclosure awards and maps, see 'Further reading'.

Estate plans

An estate plan is a large-scale plan showing the property of a single owner or corporate body such as a college. Many estate plans have accompanying terriers or books of reference in which the lands are described in detail and occupiers' or lessees' names are given. Often, especially on pre-eighteenth-century maps, locally important buildings such as churches and manor houses are shown in elevation or perspective.

Many estate plans and estate records are in local record offices, but the National Archives also has important holdings. The principal landowner represented among the public records is the Crown. The records of the Crown Estate Commissioners (CRES), the Forestry Commissioners (F), the Land Revenue Record Office (LRRO) and the Office of Works in its various guises (WORK) all contain large numbers of maps of estates which are or were formerly owned by the Crown. These maps show places which are widely scattered across the country: not only London, Hampton, Osborne, Richmond and Windsor, as one might expect, but also less obvious places such as St Columb (Cornwall), Sellindge (Kent), and Sunk Island (Yorkshire).

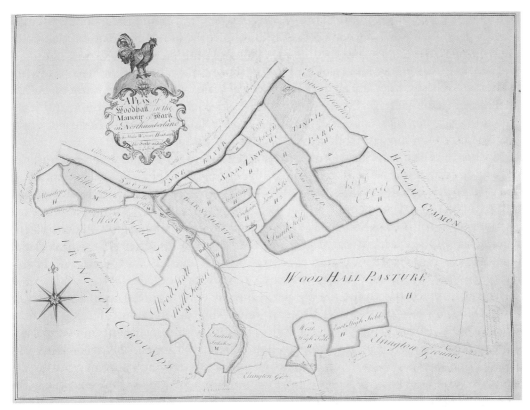

Figure 1 Plan of an estate in Woodhall, Northumberland, part of the Greenwich Hospital Northern estates which were confiscated from the Earl of Derwentwater (MPI 1/230/6, formerly part of ADM 79/13).

A major accumulation of estate plans relates to the lands of the third Earl of Derwentwater, who was executed for treason following the Rebellion of 1715. His estates were consequently forfeited to the Crown and passed in due course to Greenwich Hospital. As a result, the Hospital's records, now grouped with those of the Admiralty, include numerous plans of estates in Cumberland and Northumberland – this is a good instance of the kind of lateral thinking and historical background referred to earlier, as one would not on the face of it expect to find plans of lands on the Northumberland moors among the records of the Admiralty.

Other estate plans are among the records of the Palatinates of Chester and Durham, and of the Duchy of Lancaster. There are many plans of lands owned by such departments as the Admiralty, the Board of Ordnance, the War Office, and by the pre-nationalization railway and canal companies.

Ordnance Survey maps

The National Archives is not a place of deposit for successive editions of published Ordnance Survey maps. However, a few sets of Ordnance Survey maps are available for reference in the Map and Large Document Reading Room, principally the first ('Old Series') and second ('New Series') editions of the one-inch map, six-inch maps for a number of counties, and the five-foot plan of London.

There are very many sheets of Ordnance Survey maps among the records in the National Archives, but they are not arranged by scale, series or sheet number as they would be in a map library. If you want a specific sheet of a particular edition and scale, you may be better advised to enquire of the appropriate local studies library or of the British Library or one of the other legal deposit libraries.

Most of the Ordnance Survey maps among the records are annotated in manuscript to show information relevant to the file or paper to which they are attached, or (as in the case of the Valuation Office maps) to serve as a means of reference to some other series of records. The records of the Registrar General, for example, include an accumulation of Ordnance Survey maps marked in manuscript to show the boundaries of Registrars' Districts and Sub-Districts (**RG 18**); these are a useful means of reference both to the decennial census returns and to the records of births, marriages and deaths kept by the Office of National Statistics.

As well as producing maps, the Ordnance Survey was from 1841 responsible for the national boundary archive for Great Britain. This entailed maintaining records documenting each change to a public boundary – this included county, parish, parliamentary and local government boundaries. Although the records of the Ordnance Survey suffered much destruction as a result of enemy bombing during the Second World War, what survives is now in the National Archives and is an extensive cartographic archive of information about official boundaries of all kinds within Great Britain and how they have changed over time.

County maps and town plans

From the mid-eighteenth century onwards, many commercial mapmakers published finely engraved county maps and town plans. As well as showing place names, roads, rivers and other topographical features, many of the county maps show individual landowners' seats, names of subscribers to the map, and (usually inset) views of principal buildings, illustrations of local industries and allusions to local history.

Town plans are often very detailed and show each house and building as well as street names, rights of way, parks, public buildings etc. The Ordnance Survey five-foot plan of London already mentioned above shows the names of detached houses, the layout of gardens (paths, trees, ponds and greenhouses are all shown), the width of street pavements, what factories manufactured, the numbers of seats in churches, and even the positions of individual lamp-posts, pillar boxes and drinking-troughs for horses.

County maps and town plans are widely scattered among the records. Many are to be found among the records of the War Office (in **WO 78**, many maps from which are now in **MPH 1** and **MPHH 1**), the Land Revenue Record Office (**LRRO 1**, many maps from which are now in **MPE 1** and **MPEE 1**) and the Municipal and Parliamentary Boundaries Commission (**T 72**). Others are among the British Transport Historical

Records (**RAIL**) and the maps formerly in the Public Record Office Library (**ZMAP**). London is particularly well-represented: examples include John Rocque's map of 1747 (**ZMAP 1/40**) and Richard Horwood's map of 1799 (**ZMAP 1/41**).

Military maps

Since Tudor times, maps have been used to plan fortifications, plot defence schemes and record battles and campaigns. The National Archives holds rich accumulations of maps illustrating military and naval operations, from the sixteenth century to the Suez Campaign and the Korean War, including Blenheim, Trafalgar, Waterloo, Rorke's Drift, Passchendaele, the D-Day landings. . . . There are particularly large holdings of maps relating to the First World War, and these may be used in conjunction with other kinds of document. If you use British Army Unit War Diaries (in **WO 95**), for example, to trace the places where your grandfather or great-grandfather served, then the trench maps (in **WO 297**) will greatly increase your understanding of the situations described in the war diaries. The trench maps show the opposing trench systems in grim detail. They also enable you to identify places referred to in the war diary.

During the twentieth century, the experience of warfare was no longer restricted to members of the armed forces. Air Ministry files (**AIR 1**) include files about the earliest enemy air raids on the United Kingdom during the First World War; many of the maps showing the courses taken by enemy aircraft have been extracted from the files and are now in record series **MPI 1** or **MPII 1**. The Bomb Census Maps (**HO 193**) show where German bombs fell on the United Kingdom in the Second World War; they also provide references to reports in the Bomb Census Papers (**HO 198**).

There are also many maps and plans of buildings that an ancestor in the armed services might have known: forts, barracks, Army schools, dockyards, coastguard stations, Royal Air Force bases etc. The records of the Ordnance Office (**WO 44** and **WO 55**), the Admiralty Works Department (**ADM 140**), the Air Ministry Estates Branch (**AVIA 62**) and the Office of Works and successors (**WORK 41**, **WORK 43**, **WORK 44**) are all good sources for such plans.

Overseas

Although, as one would expect, the country most represented on maps in the National Archives is the British Isles, the Office holds very many maps of places overseas. These include not only countries which have at one time been British colonies or protectorates, but also areas in which Britain has had a commercial or strategic interest or where there have been particular diplomatic or military concerns (see above). There are maps and plans of early colonial exploration and settlement, plantations, mining concessions, cemeteries, transcontinental railways, docks, fortifications, international boundaries, battlefields, First World War trenches etc. Many land grant maps (or 'plats' as they were often called) actually record the

Figure 2a Plan of Worthy Park sugar plantation, Jamaica, owned by the Price family (MPGG 1/56/12, formerly part of CO 441/4/4): the plan shows field names and the kind of crop planted in each field. The records of the West Indian Encumbered Estates Commission include many plans of plantations and other estates.

Figure 2b View of Worthy Park sugar plantation, Jamaica (MPGG 1/56/15). Such drawings can give a vivid impression of the environment in which earlier generations lived and worked.

landowner's name on the map that shows his landholding: the records of the American Loyalists Claims Commission (**AO 13**), the East Florida Claims Commission (**T 77**) and the West Indian Encumbered Estates Commission (**CO 441**) are just three examples of series rich in such maps.

Buildings

In addition to maps strictly so called, the National Archives also holds a very large number of architectural and engineering drawings. It is probably true to say that there are examples of almost every kind of building and structure that was erected during the nineteenth and twentieth centuries. By no means every individual building is represented, but there are enough examples to enable one to form an impression of the kind of environment in which people lived and worked. One particularly rich series is the maps and plans transferred from the Ministry of Housing and Local Government (**HLG 6**), which includes plans of workhouses, hospitals, common lodging houses, museums, libraries, markets, town halls, police stations, fire stations, waterworks, even seaside bandstands. Other series containing plans of buildings are too numerous to list here: the records include plans of harbours, prisons, churches, embassies,

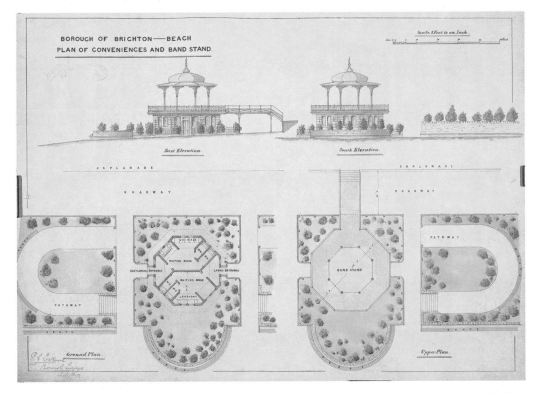

Figure 3 Design for a bandstand and public conveniences at Brighton, Sussex (HLG 6/353). The records of the Ministry of Housing and Local Government contain many drawings of buildings paid for by local authorities.

schools, lunatic asylums, railway stations, bridges, monuments, factories, coastguard stations, air-raid shelters etc.

Mapmakers

All kinds of people made maps and plans: not only professional cartographers, surveyors and architects, but also explorers, soldiers, seamen, spies, colonial administrators, town planners and civil servants. The published catalogues and the card catalogue in the Map and Large Document Reading Room contain indexes to mapmakers, both household names and obscure nobodies. Collating information from these indexes and from the maps drawn by individuals can sometimes provide a good deal of information about a person's movements and activities.

Maps and plans outside the National Archives

Many local studies libraries and local record offices have extensive holdings of maps and plans relating to the areas they serve. Local record offices may hold material from the tithe and Valuation Office surveys, enclosure awards and maps, estate plans, architectural drawings and other local records. To describe such holdings is beyond the scope of this book. Some further reading on maps and plans is suggested at the end of this book.

Introduction to the three surveys

Each of the three surveys described in this book provides a detailed snapshot of the landscape. Together, they enable us to build up a picture of change during a century of social and economic upheaval. The tithe surveys were mostly made between 1836 and about 1850, and were the most detailed examination of land use and land occupation since the Domesday Book of 1086. The extensive land and property survey carried out by the Valuation Office between 1910 and 1915, and the National Farm Survey made between 1941 and 1943, were both hailed in their time as a 'New' or 'Second' Domesday.

The maps generated by the surveys, and the textual records they were made to accompany, together provide information about individual property holders, their lands and houses and gardens. The tithe records name landowners and tenants and give the acreage and use of each parcel of titheable land. The Valuation Office records provide descriptions and plans of private houses, countryside and buildings of all kinds. The National Farm Survey paints a detailed picture of some 300,000 farms and other agricultural holdings, recording virtually every animal and fruit tree.

The records from these three surveys enable us to match people with their homes and neighbourhoods, and to learn more about the conditions under which they lived. The tithe records enable the family historian to place mid-nineteenth-century ancestors in their setting: they are contemporary with the earliest surviving census returns (from 1841 and 1851), and can supplement information about addresses obtained from the registers of births, marriages and deaths. The Valuation Office records, made half a century later, provide information about individual houses and workplaces in the period immediately before the First World War. The National Farm Survey, made during the Second World War, will be of interest if an ancestor was farming in even quite a small way. Fortunate genealogists will find three sources of information that may throw light on their ancestors and their places of abode across four generations.

Local historians will find that the records assist research into the history of particular properties, and help to form a detailed picture of urban and rural communities across time. A comparison of records from more than one survey may show changes consequent upon the Industrial Revolution and the erosion of farming land by urban development. The tithe survey gives a glimpse of rural life in early Victorian times; many of the areas shown have long since been urbanized. The Valuation Office records provide a detailed record of both urban and rural settlement in the period just before the First World War. They can also be of value in tracing public rights of way. The National Farm Survey records will enable comparisons to be made between farming conditions and rural communities during the Second World War and those of a hundred years before.

The records described in this book constitute three extensive sources of information about property ownership and land use during a period of agrarian revolution and social change. The potential for comparative historical, geographical, economic and social studies drawing on all three groups of records is enormous.

The two case studies at the end of the book, one urban and one rural, demonstrate the wealth of information about very ordinary families that can be discovered by research across these three surveys. We hope they will inspire you to use the records to learn more about your own family or locality.

2 The mid-nineteenth-century Tithe Commission

Are you researching people or places in England and Wales in about 1840? If so, tithe records may help you to find out more about them.

The records of the tithe survey show where people were living and who were their neighbours in early Victorian times. The maps are often the earliest large-scale mapping of towns and villages. Together with related textual documents, they can provide immense detail on a wide range of subjects such as crop acreage and field names, house occupancy, rights of way, parish boundaries . . .; the list goes on.

What were tithes and why was the survey needed?

Tithing was an ancient custom, by which a tenth of a farmer's yearly produce was given to support the local church and clergy. In principle, payments were to be made in kind, i.e. every tenth basket of apples, every tenth fleece of wool, every tenth bushel of wheat, was to be paid to the parish priest of the established Church for his maintenance. Such practice was cumbersome and fraught with difficulties – it must have been impossible for a clergyman to determine exactly how many eggs, for example, he was entitled to receive. Tithing became law in England as far back as the ninth century, and still existed ten centuries later, in many places scarcely changed. By the early nineteenth century, however, against a background of industrialization, religious dissent and agricultural depression, tithe was a very unpopular anachronism. It unfairly penalized farmers, since manufactured goods were not subject to tithes, and was resented by the growing body of nonconformists, who thus had to support the established church as well as their own. It discouraged agricultural improvement, since farmers put in capital investment, risk and hard work only then to pay part of the resulting profit to tithe owners. In many cases, the link between church and tithes had been broken as far back as the Reformation. The tithe payer often found himself paying a large proportion of his produce to an unknown person or institution, and receiving nothing in return. The tithe owners found it tiresome and difficult to assess and collect tithe in kind, and to store perishable foodstuffs.

In many parishes, monetary payments came to be substituted for payments in kind. This substitution was called commutation. The Enclosure Acts of the eighteenth and early nineteenth centuries were often a catalyst for extinguishing the obligation to pay tithes in kind. This explains why there are relatively few places for which there exist both tithe and enclosure records. However, enclosure only affected some areas, and the great majority of parishes in England and Wales were still paying tithes in kind by the

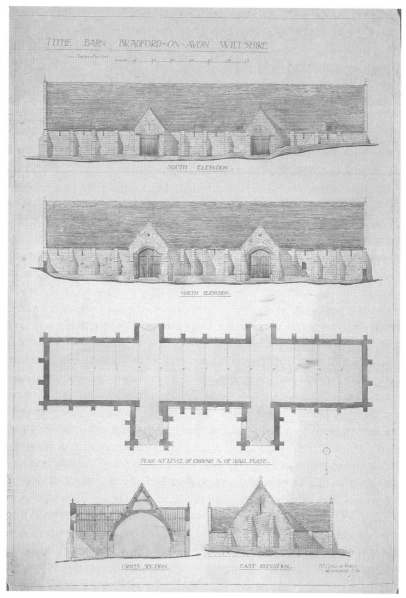

Figure 4 Plan and elevation of the massive medieval tithe barn at Bradford on Avon, Wiltshire, used to store grain collected as 'tithes in kind' (WORK 31/888). The barn is now in the care of English Heritage.

early nineteenth century. It was clear that a more far-reaching initiative was needed.

By the early 1830s there was widespread agricultural depression and tithes were a focus for rural unrest. In 1836, Parliament passed the Tithe Commutation Act, which aimed to replace all remaining tithes in kind in England and Wales by more convenient money payments; the Act called these payments tithe rentcharge. Tithe rentcharge was to be paid by all affected parishioners in proportion to the amount of land they held.

How and when was the survey carried out?

The administration of the Act was overseen by tithe commissioners in London, while assistant tithe commissioners and local agents carried out the practical work 'in the field'. It was first necessary to ascertain the extent of existing tithe commutation and of the circumstances of each district where tithes were still being paid in kind. Then the land had to be surveyed and valued, usually by local men, to arrive at total parish rentcharge figures. Finally, each individual landowner's liability had to be calculated. The assistant tithe commissioners travelled to all parts of the country to hold meetings with parishioners about valuations, and to settle the terms of the commutation of their tithes. These terms were formalized in a document called a tithe agreement, if all parties concurred, or a tithe award, if the assistant commissioner had to arbitrate in a dispute (although in some cases there was no real dispute; it was merely that the amount of tithe to be paid was so small that landowners waited for the assistant commissioner to take the initiative in sorting it out). The agreement or award formed the basis of the tithe apportionment, which is the legal document setting out landowners' individual liabilities. Each apportionment was accompanied by a map which served as the means of reference to the plot numbers given on the apportionment. Both the map and the apportionment were signed by the tithe commissioners. A tithe apportionment and map technically constitute a single document, but for convenience of use and storage they were separated long before their transfer to the Public Record Office (now the National Archives) and so now form two record series.

Once the arrangements had been approved by all parties and the commissioners, tithe rentcharge became payable in lieu of tithe in kind. However, disagreements about the terms of commutation, refusals to pay for making the required maps, and a shortage of trained surveyors all meant that the survey took a long time to complete. Although most districts were mapped by 1850, a handful of cases dragged on into the 1860s and 1870s. The last tithe apportionment and map to be made were not completed until 1883; they relate to part of the parish of Hemingstone in Suffolk.

These records were not a final statement, set in stone. As land ownership changed over the decades, often reflecting wider social developments such as urbanization and the advent of the railway, these changes were recorded by the creation of altered apportionments and maps, limited to the area affected. There were minor amendments to the system during the nineteenth century, and the Tithe Commission's functions passed to other bodies. By the twentieth century, the concept of tithe was more anachronistic than ever; the Tithe Act of 1936 started winding up the system, by replacing rentcharge with redemption annuities payable for sixty years. Owing to the high cost of administering these, they were extinguished in 1977, when the last ever tithe payments were made. There is no longer any tithe liability as such.

This guide is concerned primarily with the records generated by the Tithe Commutation Act 1836. If you wish to try to trace the story of a tithe area further, using records available at the National Archives, you should refer to Domestic Information Leaflet 41 *Tithe Records*.

Records of the Tithe Commission

The principal series of records of the tithe survey held by the National Archives are:

- tithe **apportionments** (in record series **IR 29**) which provide a record of names of landowners and occupiers, of land use and tithe rentcharge
- tithe **maps** (in record series **IR 30**) showing the numbered tithe plots; the Tithe Commission called such plots 'tithe areas'
- tithe **files** (in **IR 18**) containing the surviving working papers of the tithe commissioners.

Most researchers will look at both the map and the apportionment for their parish, perhaps looking at one of them first, depending on why they are making a search in the tithe records; or perhaps looking at them both together.

Researchers may use these records because:

- they are interested in a particular individual or family living in a given parish
- they wish to find out about a particular property
- they are interested in a locality
- they require a large-scale map of an area in the mid-nineteenth-century, in which case they may need to use the apportionment as a key to the features shown.

Those looking for individuals will need to start by finding the relevant tithe apportionment, in which names are listed. Note the plot number in the column against any names in which you are interested (see illustration on p.25), and then look at the map to see where these plot numbers were located.

The first step for most other researchers is usually to find the relevant tithe map. Local historians may wish to get an overall picture of their parish from the map, before looking at the detail provided by the apportionment, and any surviving papers in the tithe file. Those interested in a particular building or piece of land will need to look at the tithe map to locate the property in which they are interested, make a note of its plot number and then identify the appropriate entry in the apportionment.

The tithe apportionments and maps are arranged in separate series, alphabetically by the (old) counties of England and then by those of Wales. Hampshire was designated as the county of Southampton and so appears between Somerset and Staffordshire. Monmouthshire was included in England, not Wales.

Within each county there is an alphabetical arrangement of the tithe districts (i.e. districts subject to tithe commutation). A tithe district was one in which tithes were paid separately from the surrounding areas. In most cases this is the same area as an ecclesiastical parish, or a township in large northern parishes; it might also be a hamlet, chapelry, manor, liberty, tithing or extra-parochial place. Occasionally tithe districts were formed from parts of parishes where tithe was paid separately; in these cases, there may be an entry in the series list for the district where tithe was payable, but not for the main parish. Upper Heyford parish in Northamptonshire was divided into three tithe districts, each titheable to a different parish – Bugbrook, Flore and Lower Heyford. To make matters even more confusing, two of those three parishes also have separate tithe maps.

The districts are listed using the original order given to them by the tithe commissioners, which is alphabetical. However, you may not find your place listed where you might expect, for a number of reasons. You may need to search the online catalogue or look through the whole of the paper series list for your county to find your district (see the section on how to find and use the tithe maps, p.22), especially if your place has two or more words as part of the name. Generally, words such as 'Great', 'Little', 'North', 'Over' and 'S[ain]t' were disregarded as far as alphabetical order was concerned, so although Much Marcle appears in the M section for Herefordshire, so too does Little Marcle; both are listed between Mansell Lacy and Marden. Over Wyresdale in Lancashire is listed under W; St Just in Roseland, Cornwall, under J. However, not all first words were disregarded; where they were considered more substantive, they determine where the place was listed. Thus, King's Sutton in Northamptonshire appears under K, English Bicknor in Gloucestershire under E, and Spittle Hill township in Northumberland under S. If you are looking for a small place in the north, note that township names were not formed in alphabetical order, so the township of Netherwasdale, Eskdale and Wasdale in Cumberland appears under N, and is not cross-referenced from E or W. Where a tithe district had been formed, such as the district of Octon Grange in the parish of Thwing in Yorkshire, this district will usually be listed under its own name, rather than that of the parish. In this case, there is no entry for the parish of Thwing itself, so a researcher looking for a property within Thwing would need to search the online catalogue for 'Thwing' and 'IR 30' to find reference to the district of Octon Grange, or look through the whole of the series list for the West Riding of Yorkshire.

The document references for the apportionment and map for a place are the same except for the **IR 29** or **IR 30** designation. They consist of county and parish numbers added to these series. Thus the apportionment for Kew, Surrey, is held under the reference **IR 29/34/74**, and the map reference is **IR 30/34/74**.

There are no tithe maps and apportionments for some places, although a tithe file was opened for every tithe district, regardless of whether tithe was still payable there. This may be because tithes in the district had already been dealt with as part of the enclosure process. However, not all enclosures commuted tithes, and there are some instances in which there are both enclosure and tithe records. Sometimes, too, enclosure occurred later than tithe commutation, although this is rare; Cambridgeshire is one county where this was more common. There are also no maps and apportionments for areas where no tithe was payable. There are less likely to be tithe records for urban areas, although you should bear in mind that many areas which are now towns were then much less urban. Some counties were more affected by tithe commutation than others: there are fewer records for the extensively enclosed midland counties, and for Westmorland, Lancashire and Gloucestershire, while other counties, especially in western districts and Wales, were almost entirely covered. However, there are maps and apportionments for 11,785 tithe districts, around 75 % of England and Wales.

Three copies were to be made of each tithe apportionment and tithe map: one for the Tithe Commission, one for the diocesan records representing the interests of the tithe owner; and one to be kept in the parish chest, for the tithe payers' use. All copies were signed, and sealed where applicable, by the commissioners. The apportionments and maps held by the National Archives are those which were in the custody of the tithe commissioners. The copies which were deposited with the registrar of the diocese and in the parish church are often now among the holdings of local record offices. Researchers who live in England, but at a distance from London, may be well advised first to consult their local record office to see if they hold copies of the tithe maps and apportionments for their area, and any altered apportionments and maps. Researchers in Wales may prefer to visit the National Library of Wales, which holds copies of the Welsh maps and apportionments. Other documents of the Tithe Commission such as the tithe files are available only at the National Archives at Kew.

Scotland and Ireland

Tithe files, maps and apportionments held at the National Archives relate to England and Wales only. For their equivalent in Scotland, Northern Ireland and the Republic of Ireland you are advised to contact the relevant national record office.

The equivalent of tithes in Scotland were 'teinds'. These were payable by the owners of heritable property within a parish, at first in kind and then by money. The system was never a burden on the land as it was in England and Wales, and there was no Scottish equivalent of the Tithe Commutation Act 1836 and no resulting land survey. The system of teinds was ended by Act of Parliament in 1925. The National Archives of Scotland holds records of the Teind Court and Commissioners in its record classes TE 1–6 (pre-1700), and TE 7–32 (post-1700). Records of teinds are also found amongst private and estate records.

For Ireland, the Tithe Applotment Books compiled between 1823 and 1838 are in the custody of the Public Record Office of Northern Ireland (FIN/5A) and the National Archives, Dublin.

The tithe maps (IR 30)

The maps provide a graphic index to the apportionments, using numbers to link each plot of land shown on the map to its description in the apportionment.

The tithe commissioners at first tried to secure a uniform standard for the maps that were to illustrate the tithe apportionment, so that they might form the basis for a national cadastral survey. Lieutenant Robert K. Dawson, a Royal Engineer officer, had been appointed to superintend the surveys, and he endeavoured to impose a uniformity of scale and conventional signs. Dawson's recommendations were published for Parliament: a copy of his recommended conventional signs is available in the Map and Large Document Reading Room (in a folder labelled 'Tithe Key').

Since the expense of the surveys was to be paid by the landowners, however, the tithe commissioners had to retreat from insisting upon maps meeting this ideal standard. The amending Tithe Act 1837 provided that any map might be used for the purposes of tithe commutation, provided it was accepted by at least two-thirds of the landowners in the parish. This amendment resulted in a great variety of style and scale among the tithe maps. Some tithe districts were mapped in their entirety, while others were only mapped for those parts subject to tithe commutation. To save the cost of making a new survey, existing maps were sometimes used or copied. The size of the maps varies considerably: some are enormous, up to 14 feet wide and of a comparable length, while others, perhaps just concerned with a few fields, may measure only one foot by two feet. The scales most widely used for the maps range between one inch to three chains and one inch to six chains (one inch to three chains is equivalent to about 25 inches to one mile). Most maps are manuscript, drawn on parchment. A few of the maps are lithographs, mostly produced by Standidge and Company; this may be the case where the requirement for extra copies made lithography a cheaper option than copying by hand, or where it had been decided to sell copies to the public to recoup the expense of making the map.

The fact that the 1837 Act allowed maps of varying standards to be submitted to the Tithe Commission meant that the tithe commissioners were not able to certify that they were all accurate, as the 1836 Act required them to do. An amendment to the 1837 Act resolved this dilemma by allowing the commissioners to certify only those maps with whose accuracy they were satisfied. The amendment provided for two classes of maps. 'First-class maps' were those which the commissioners considered sufficiently accurate to serve as legal evidence of boundaries and land plots; there are 1,900 of these maps, only about 16% of the total. These maps can be identified by the fact that they bear the seal of the Tithe Commission and a certificate of accuracy signed by two

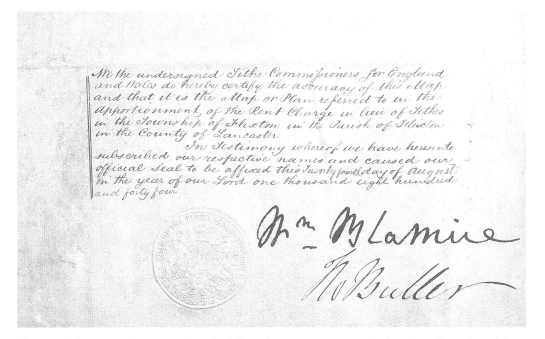

Figure 5 The certification and seal of the tithe commissioners, indicating a first-class tithe map. From the tithe map of the township of Flixton in Lancashire (IR 30/18/127).

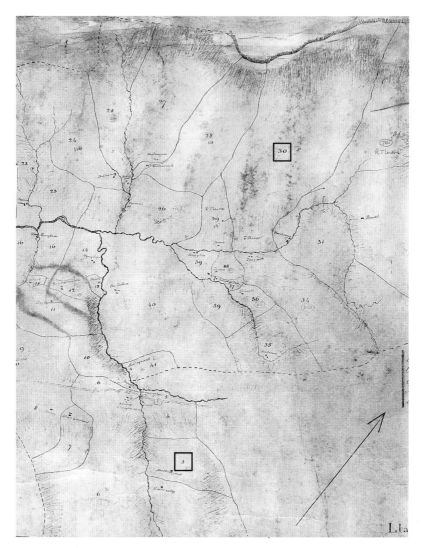

Figure 6 The tithe map of Llanfihangel, Merionethshire, was apparently drawn by a surveyor standing on top of a mountain; the relative positions of the plots are correct, but the proportions of the plots are distorted by perspective (IR 30/52/24).

commissioners. The 'second-class maps', as the remaining maps are called, vary in accuracy, from those which narrowly missed a first-class seal, to those which are patently unreliable. For example, some Welsh surveyors were reputed to have climbed the local mountain and simply drawn what they could see, with the result that the fields nearer to the mountain are drawn larger than those at a distance, regardless of the relative acreage shown in the apportionment.

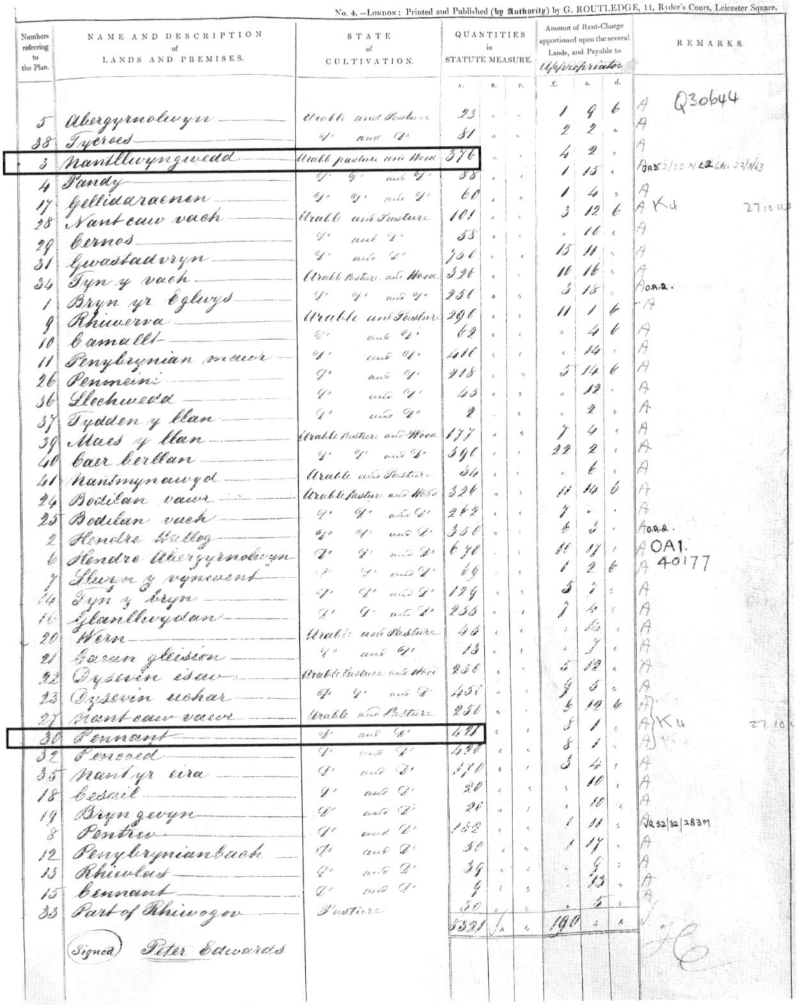

No. 4.—London: Printed and Published (by Authority) by G. ROUTLEDGE, 11, Ryder's Court, Leicester Square.

Numbers referring to the Plan.	NAME AND DESCRIPTION of LANDS AND PREMISES.	STATE of CULTIVATION.	QUANTITIES in STATUTE MEASURE. A.	R.	P.	Amount of Rent-Charge apportioned upon the several Lands, and Payable to Appropriator £.	s.	d.	REMARKS.
5	Abergyrnolwyn	Arable and Pasture	23	.	.	1	9	6	A Q30644
38	Tyeroes	Do and Do	81	.	.	2	2	.	A
3	Nantllwyngwedd	Arable pasture and Wood	376	.	.	4	2	.	A
4	Pandy	Do Do and Do	88	.	.	1	15	.	A OA52/32 NL2 Ch. 22/3/63
17	Gellidaraenen	Do Do and Do	60	.	.	1	4	.	A
28	Nant cau vach	Arable and Pasture	101	.	.	3	12	6	A Ku 27 10
29	Cernos	Do and Do	58	.	.	.	16	.	A
31	Gwastadvryn	Do and Do	750	.	.	15	11	.	A
34	Tyn y vach	Arable Pasture and Wood	326	.	.	10	16	.	A
1	Bryn yr Eglwys	Do Do and Do	251	.	.	3	18	.	A O.A.2.
9	Rhiwerva	Arable and Pasture	290	.	.	11	1	6	A
10	Camallt	Do and Do	62	.	.	.	4	6	A
11	Penybryniau mawr	Do and Do	416	.	.	.	14	.	A
26	Penmeini	Do and Do	218	.	.	5	14	6	A
36	Llechwedd	Do and Do	45	.	.	.	12	.	A
37	Tydden y llan	Do and Do	2	.	.	.	2	.	A
39	Maes y llan	Arable Pasture and Wood	177	.	.	7	4	.	A
40	Caer berllan	Do Do and Do	590	.	.	22	2	.	A
41	Nantmynawyd	Arable and Pasture	34	.	.	.	6	.	A
24	Bodilan vawr	Arable Pasture and Wood	326	.	.	11	14	6	A
25	Bodilan vach	Do Do and Do	262	.	.	7	.	.	A
2	Hendre Hallog	Do Do and Do	350	.	.	6	3	.	A O.A.2.
6	Hendre Abergyrnolwyn	Do Do and Do	670	.	.	11	17	.	A OA1. 40177
7	Llwyn y rynnwent	Do Do and Do	69	.	.	1	2	6	A
14	Tyn y bryn	Do Do and Do	129	.	.	5	7	.	A
16	Glanllwydan	Do Do and Do	235	.	.	7	4	.	A
20	Wern	Arable and Pasture	46	.	.	.	16	.	A
21	Garan gleision	Do and Do	13	.	.	.	7	.	A
22	Dysevin isaf	Arable Pasture and Wood	250	.	.	5	12	.	A
23	Dysevin uchar	Do Do and Do	455	.	.	9	5	.	A
27	Nant cau vawr	Arable and Pasture	250	.	.	6	12	6	A } Ku 27.10
30	Pennant	Do and Do	411	.	.	8	1	.	A
32	Pencoed	Do and Do	498	.	.	8	1	.	A
35	Nant yr eira	Do and Do	370	.	.	3	4	.	A
18	Cesail	Do and Do	20	.	.	.	10	.	A
19	Bryn gwyn	Do and Do	20	.	.	.	10	.	A
8	Pentre	Do and Do	182	.	.	1	11	.	A VQ52/32/283M
12	Penybryniau bach	Do and Do	50	.	.	1	17	.	A
13	Rhiwlas	Do and Do	39	.	.	.	9	.	A
15	Cennant	Do and Do	9	.	.	.	13	.	A
33	Part of Rhiwogov	Pasture	30	.	.	.	5	.	A
			5321	.	.	190	.	.	

(Signed) Peter Edwards

Figure 7 The tithe apportionment for Llanfihangel (IR 29/52/24) gives field areas which bear little relation to the sizes of plots as shown on the tithe map: compare the apportionment entries for plots 3 and 30 with the depiction of these plots on the map opposite.

What do the tithe maps show?

The primary function of the tithe maps was to provide a means of reference to the apportionments. Each piece of land liable to tithes was depicted and given a number, unique within the tithe district, by which it could be identified in the apportionment.

Some maps show little more than this bare requirement, although they all show the outer boundaries of the tithe district, as well as the boundaries of the tithe plots within districts. Other maps are works of art, whether they conform to Dawson's recommendations (as Peasmarsh in Sussex) or not (as New Brentford, Middlesex, shown on the cover of this book). The amount of detail shown on tithe maps is very variable. Most maps show roads, waterways, and at least some buildings, and woodland is often shown. Occasionally one finds information noted about hedges, field names, mines and factories. Maps of plots which had not been enclosed may show pre-enclosure field systems in detail. The boundaries of unenclosed lands are often shown by dotted lines, whereas those of enclosed lands are generally represented by continuous lines. The name of the surveyor is often given, perhaps with his signature; there may be a scale bar and a compass indicator.

Although sometimes hard to interpret, the tithe maps represent the earliest large-scale mapping of most of the parishes of England and Wales, and are an invaluable resource for local historians. They often demand considerable local knowledge of the landscape, and reference to more modern maps of the area. After 1936 the Tithe Redemption Commission began a programme of marking Ordnance Survey maps with the boundaries and plot numbers of tithe areas; these maps, known as district record maps, are in **IR 90**.

It should be borne in mind that it was not only rural landscapes that were subject to tithes. Gardens and smaller plots of pasture within an urban context were often titheable, so many urban areas are depicted in detail. The expansion of many cities was to take place within a few years of the tithe surveys, and the tithe maps serve as a major record of a landscape of fields and woods soon to be overrun by brick and stone.

How to find and use the tithe maps in IR 30

There are a number of ways to find your tithe map reference. They apply equally to finding a tithe apportionment (**IR 29**).

1. A research project undertaken by the University of Exeter examined all the tithe maps in detail, and the results of that project were published by Roger Kain and Richard Oliver. Each tithe map is listed with information about its content, conventional signs, scale, date and maker. Where a map shows only the titheable part of a district, rather than a whole parish or township, this is noted. A copy is available for consultation in the Map and Large Document Reading Room; note that you need to add the series number 'IR 30' to the two numbers given in this book for your parish, to get your complete document ordering reference. For an apportionment reference, substitute 'IR 29' for 'IR 30'. The Kain and Oliver publication gives the date of the apportionment, where known.

2. If you are at the National Archives, you can also use the paper series list for IR 29 and IR 30 to find the document reference for your parish.

3. If you wish to obtain your map reference before or during your visit via the online catalogue (PROCAT), you can easily find the reference using the search facility, putting in the name of the parish in Field 1, and the series 'IR 30' in Field 3, then pressing the 'Search' button.

PROCAT

1. You must type in a word or phrase. You can search for more than one by typing AND to link them.

> Down St Mary

2. You may also select a year or range of years: e.g. 1805 [to] 1805; 1914 [to] 1918.

> ___ to ___

3. You may also select part of the catalogue, if you know a department code (e.g. FO) or series reference (e.g. OS 35). Separate two or more entries such as FO, DO 5, using a comma.

> IR 30

4. (search)

Search Results

You ran a basic search on "Down St Mary" restricted to reference(s): IR 30.
There was **1** hit on the Catalogue.

PRO Reference	Title/Scope and Content	Covering Dates
IR 30/9/160	Down, St Mary (P)	

4. If you do not know the name of the tithe district in which your property lay, begin by consulting the relevant county sheet in the set of County Diagrams (Key Sheets), which are kept in the central map reference cabinet in the Map and Large Document Reading Room. These sheets are reduced photocopies of Ordnance Survey index maps, to which have been added (in manuscript) information about tithe districts.

The key sheets are in three volumes, arranged in alphabetical order of county name, as follows:

Volume 1: Bedfordshire – Norfolk
Volume 2: Northamptonshire – Yorkshire (including Hampshire as 'Southampton')
Volume 3: Wales: Anglesey – Radnorshire

In these volumes, the index maps for each county are coloured in yellow to show the tithe districts subject to the Tithe Commutation Act. The county number appears in the top right-hand corner of the diagram sheet. Small red numbers in the centre of a parish provide the tithe district number, completing a document reference of IR 30/county number/parish number. Generally parishes where tithes had been commuted by enclosure are coloured pink: there is no tithe apportionment or map for these places.

You will then want to see your tithe map, once you have found the correct reference for it. The tithe maps have been copied to microfiche for preservation reasons, for English counties alphabetically up to and including Middlesex; readers requiring maps for these counties normally consult the microfiche copies available on open

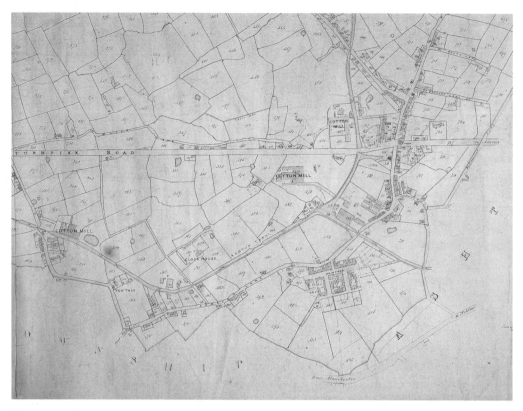

Figure 8 The tithe map of Droylesden, now part of Manchester (IR 30/18/106). Urban features were already evident in 1847: note the canal, turnpike roads, toll house, cotton mills, and the Moravian settlement of Fairfield.

access in the Map and Large Document Reading Room. For English counties alphabetically from Monmouthshire to Yorkshire and all Welsh counties, you will need to order the original map. It will normally be a rolled map; if it is particularly large or you are unsure how to handle it, please ask staff for assistance.

You may then wish to look at the corresponding apportionment to see the written information about the area shown on the map.

Tithe Maps Supplementary (IR 77)

Some tithe maps were so heavily used that they fell into a bad state of disrepair. In most of these cases, the maps were copied by the Ministry of Agriculture and Fisheries, to whose custody they had passed in 1919, and it is these copies which are now in **IR 30**. The originals are in the series of Tithe Maps Supplementary (**IR 77**). They number about one hundred, and Middlesex, Essex, Kent, and Surrey maps are represented in particular. They are in poor condition, and are unfit for production; they may only be consulted as a last resort, when the maps in **IR 30** demonstrably provide an inadequate reproduction. The volume on tithe maps by Kain and Oliver notes where the original is held in **IR 77**.

The tithe apportionments (IR 29)

The tithe apportionment was the main record of how tithes were to be commuted, showing how the overall rentcharge for the district was apportioned to individual landowners on the basis of identifiable pieces of land. It recorded details of the numbered tithe plots and the tithe rentcharge fixed upon them, so that it was clear how much each tithe payer had to pay the tithe owner. The apportionments were normally handwritten on parchment sheets, but were sometimes printed, mainly for districts in Cornwall, Devon, Kent and Suffolk.

These documents are standard in format and content. They begin with a statement of the articles of agreement between the landowners and the tithe owners or the terms of the award imposed by the tithe commissioners. They give summary information about the parish, such as the total area, the name(s) of the tithe owner(s), and the acreage of titheable and non-titheable lands (commons, roads, Crown lands, etc.). If land was exempt from tithe, information will be given about it here. Next follows the schedule of apportionment giving details of each individual tithe area, which is set out in eight columns showing: landowners, occupiers, plot number, name and description of lands and premises, state of cultivation, quantities in acres, roods and perches (40 perches equal 1 rood and 4 roods equal 1 acre); amount of rentcharge assessed, and remarks.

LANDOWNERS.	OCCUPIERS.	Numbers referring to the Plan.	NAME AND DESCRIPTION or LANDS AND PREMISES.	STATE or CULTIVATION.	Quantities in Statute Measure.	Amount of Rent-charge appurtioned to the several Lands and payable to the Rector.	REMARKS.

The apportionment finishes with a summary of the schedule, which lists the landowners alphabetically by surname; names occupiers of their holdings (not listed alphabetically, but usually by the size of the land held); and adds up the rentcharge on individual properties to the global figure due from each landowner to the tithe owner.

You should therefore be able to discover for each tithe area the name of the landowner, the name of the occupier if this was a different person, the type of property, whether the land was ploughed or laid to grass, its area and extent, the amount of rentcharge paid, and to whom.

How to find and use the tithe apportionments

If you have already found the reference for the relevant tithe map, you can find the reference for the apportionment by taking the last two numbers and adding 'IR 29' before them, instead of 'IR 30'. If you do not have the reference, you can get it by using the same means as described in 'How to find and use tithe maps' (p. 22).

The apportionments are accessed on microfilm in the Map and Large Document Reading Room. The officer-in-charge of the reading room should be consulted for requests to see an original map in cases where the film is unclear or where distinctions made by different colours are vital for the interpretation of the map or of notes in the Remarks column. Please note that the original documents are stored off-site, and you will need to allow three days for them to be brought to Kew.

In even an average-sized parish, there are likely to be several hundred plot numbers, running to a dozen or more pages of apportionment. The arrangement is not by plot number in consecutive order, however, but usually by surname of landowner. In districts where there was a major landowner, he was sometimes listed first, especially if he was titled.

If you are interested in a place, you will probably have already looked at the tithe map and found your place and the unique plot number attached to it. Look up this number in the key at the front of the apportionment, to find on which page this plot number is listed. You will there find the details, including ownership and occupation, and the size and use of all the plots of land.

If you are looking for a person, it is easiest to start with the summary of the schedule, which follows the schedule itself. If you find a name of interest, you can then turn to the details in the main body of the apportionment.

Annotations in tithe apportionments

The last column of the apportionment, 'Remarks', was often used to add in abbreviated form information about the later history of the tithe rentcharge. Table 1 explains the most frequently encountered annotations in the tithe apportionments and tells you where to find the records to which they relate. Further annotations sometimes found in the description column are the pencilled letters A or N; these indicate agricultural and non-agricultural respectively, and relate to the calculation of redemption annuities. If you find any abbreviations not listed in Table 1, a key is available from the officer on duty in the Map and Large Document Reading Room.

Altered apportionments

Most places have experienced changes in the way land has been divided up. When such changes affected the proportion of tithe rentcharge to be paid, this may be recorded in an altered apportionment and map, which document only the area of change, and not the whole parish. A very common cause of such altered apportionments was the construction of a railway through the parish. Some parishes may have several altered apportionments, if they were affected by urbanization and the growth of railways.

The altered apportionments are numbered serially in order of date, and this number may be quoted in the annotation in the 'Remarks' column of the original

Annotation	Meaning	Where to look next
AA	Altered apportionment	Altered apportionments are laced up with the original apportionments in **IR 29**. The related maps may be attached to the apportionments or detached and rolled with the original tithe map in **IR 30**.
CR	Compulsory redemption of tithe rent charge or tithe redemption annuity	The 1936 Act made it compulsory to redeem tithe rentcharge liability of less than £1; in 1958, this figure was increased to £3. Only a small sample of records of compulsory redemption has been preserved: these are in **IR 900**.
CRA	Corn rent annuity: corn rents were usually created by an enclosure award	Where the corn rent was redeemed, the redemption money was payable in the form of an annuity; redemption certificates, which specify the terms of redemption, are in **IR 108**. Only a small sample of records relating to corn rent annuities has been preserved: these are in **IR 900**. Altered apportionments of corn rents are in **IR 107**.
KA	Voluntary redemption of tithe redemption annuity	Tithe plot numbers and date of redemption may be established from **IR 94**. Redeemers' names are not given.
M	Merger	Declarations of merger are in **TITH 3**. These are found particularly in cases where the landowners were themselves the tithe owners; an agreement or award of gross tithe rentcharge was often followed by the merger of the tithe rentcharge.
OA	Order for apportionment of tithe redemption annuity	Orders for apportionment are in **IR 94**, and are similar to altered apportionments of tithe rentcharge. The related maps are usually filed with the orders, but are occasionally to be found in **IR 90**.
R	Redemption of tithe rentcharge by lump sum	Registers of certificates of redemption are in **IR 109**. Redeemers' names are not given.
RA	Redemption of tithe rentcharge by annuity	Certificates of redemption are in **IR 102**. Redeemers' names are not given.

Table 1 The most frequently encountered annotations in the tithe apportionments.

apportionment. The usual means of numbering new plots created by the subdivision of an existing plot was to add letters to the original plot number; so that plot 231 might be divided to become 231a, 231b, etc. Some parishes have no altered apportionments: this does not necessarily mean that no change took place; it may have simply been that informal and local agreements were made between the tithe owners and landowners.

Until 1936, altered apportionments were sewn up with the original apportionment, and will therefore be found in **IR 29**. The related maps will usually be found with the altered apportionments, unless they were large, in which case they are usually to be found with the tithe map in **IR 30**. After 1936, the equivalent of altered apportionments were filed separately, and called Orders for Apportionment; these are in **IR 94**.

Altered apportionments can help to cross the time bridge between about 1840 and 1910 or even sometimes into the 1920s and 1930s. The altered apportionments show only the areas of change, but are a valuable supplementary source for the local historian. For example, Down St Mary, Devon, had three altered apportionments: the earliest showed the advent of the railway, and the latest showed the acquisition of land by the county council. In addition to showing changes in land use, altered apportionments can sometimes enable us to learn about later landowners. Because they usually only show small areas of land, it is rare for altered apportionments to be helpful for family historians. You may be lucky, however: the second Down St Mary altered apportionment does show a change which affected the May family. (See Down St Mary case study, Chapter 6.)

The tithe files (IR 18)

A file was opened for each tithe district in England and Wales, even for the districts where tithe was already extinguished (no longer payable). These files form the series **IR 18**. They are listed by county and tithe district: use the online catalogue to search, or consult the paper list. The correct ordering format is IR 18 + number. For the Kew tithe file the document reference is **IR 18/10153**. Some files consist of the cover and nothing else; this may be because the files were heavily 'weeded' in the early twentieth century. Files for districts where tithe was no longer payable usually contain little more than a brief statement by a Tithe Commission official to confirm that all tithes had been extinguished. In other files, especially in cases of dispute about the tithe process, there is often substantial information which illustrates the administrative process by which tithe was commuted, and which may be of interest to local and family historians. There may be a variety of correspondence; draft agreements, awards and maps; and minutes of meetings about the commutation process. Some of the documents are written on pre-printed forms, of which perhaps the most useful for local historians is the assistant commissioner's report. There is no set order of arrangement of papers within the tithe files, but it is generally chronological, perhaps starting with a confirmation that sufficient advance notice had been given of the first public meeting, and ending with an acknowledgement that the parish and diocesan copies of the tithe map and apportionment had been received. If there was a later altered apportionment (see p. 26), there may be papers concerning this.

What kind of information can the tithe records provide for family and local historians?

The majority of the tithe maps and apportionments were made within a decade of 1841, the date of the first population census from which the returns survive. They can be used to learn more about people and places at that time.

Information about people

Tithe owners

They are identified in the preamble to the apportionment. Sometimes, the tithes were divided between two or even three tithe owners. In many cases the tithe owner was the rector of the parish or an ecclesiastical body, such as a monastery, bishop or prior (an ecclesiastical tithe owner was known as an appropriator), or a lay person or institution such as a school or college (a secular tithe owner was known as an impropriator). Where the rector was not a clergyman, he would normally appoint a vicar to carry out his parochial services, for which the vicar would be given some part of the tithes in return. Many tithe owners were public schools, Oxbridge colleges or members of the aristocracy, and therefore were far removed from the people who actually paid the tithes.

When the tithe owner actually lived in the parish, he will also be listed in the schedule of the apportionment as owner or occupier. An example is the case of the Reverend Patrick Brontë, who is listed in the Haworth apportionment as occupier of the parsonage. The Haworth tithes, however, were payable not to him but to the vicar of Bradford.

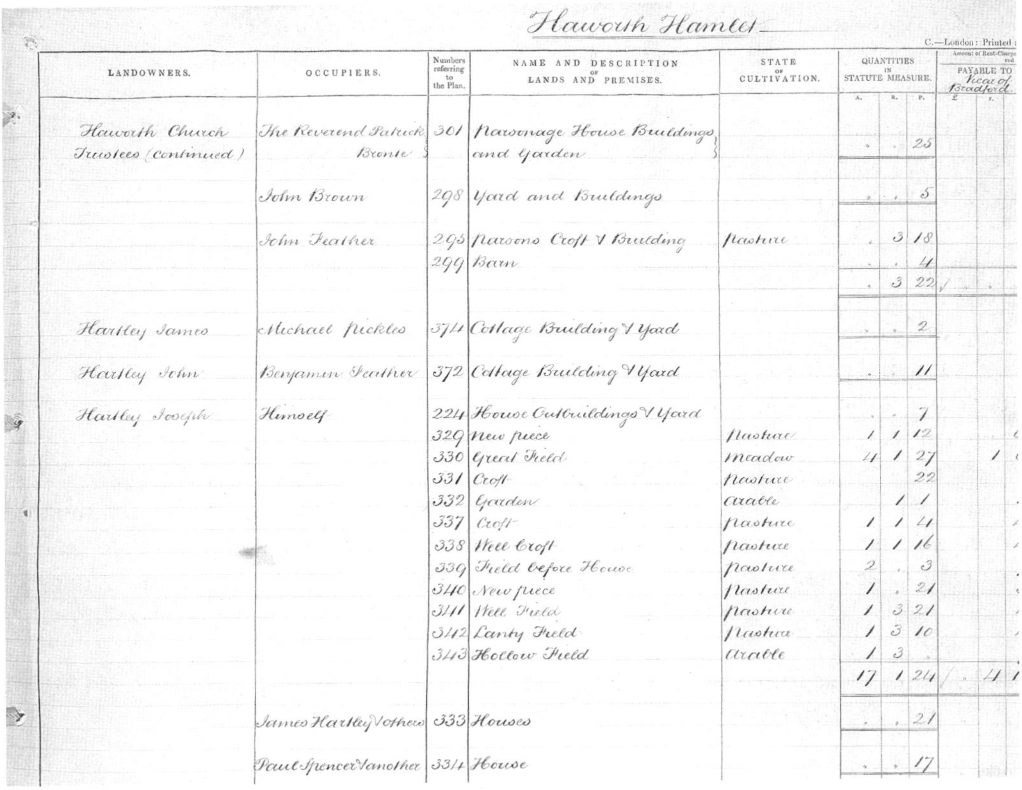

Haworth Hamlet

C.—London: Printed

LANDOWNERS.	OCCUPIERS.	Numbers referring to the Plan.	NAME AND DESCRIPTION OF LANDS AND PREMISES.	STATE OF CULTIVATION.	QUANTITIES IN STATUTE MEASURE. A.	R.	P.	Amount of Rent-Charge ... PAYABLE TO Vicar of Bradford. £	s.
Haworth Church Trustees (continued)	The Reverend Patrick Bronte	301	Parsonage House Buildings and Garden		.	.	25		
	John Brown	298	Yard and Buildings		.	.	5		
	John Feather	295	Parsons Croft & Building	Pasture	.	3	18		
		299	Barn		.	.	4		
					.	3	22	.	.
Hartley James	Michael Pickles	374	Cottage Building & Yard		.	.	2		
Hartley John	Benjamin Feather	372	Cottage Building & Yard		.	.	11		
Hartley Joseph	Himself	224	House Outbuildings & Yard		.	.	7		
		329	New piece	Pasture	1	1	12		
		330	Great Field	Meadow	4	1	27		1
		331	Croft	Pasture			22		
		332	Garden	Arable		1	1		
		337	Croft	Pasture	1	1	4		
		338	Well Croft	Pasture	1	1	16		
		339	Field before House	Pasture	2	.	3		
		340	New piece	Pasture	1	.	21		
		341	Well Field	Pasture	1	3	21		
		342	Lanty Field	Pasture	1	3	10		
		343	Hollow Field	Arable	1	3	.		
					17	1	24	.	4
	James Hartley & others	333	Houses		.	.	21		
	Paul Spencer & another	334	House		.	.	17		

Figure 9 The tithe apportionment for Haworth shows the Reverend Patrick Brontë (father of the novelists Charlotte, Emily and Anne Brontë) as occupier of the parsonage (IR 29/43/200).

Landowners

The tithe survey gives information on most landowners in a parish, rather than the narrow single-family focus of estate surveys. The Tithe Commission did not investigate the legal basis for claimed ownership, but since owners paid the expenses of commutation, it seems likely that those claiming ownership were those who either were in actual possession of the land, or received rent or profits from it. This may include those who did not own the land outright, but who had a tenancy for life or long lease; there is often an explanation given in these cases. For instance, in the Down St Mary example, Robert May is listed as owner of one farm, occupier of another, and owner (lessee) of a third farm. (See Figure 30a, p. 93.)

Occupiers

The tithe survey provides names of occupiers, and shows the land occupied and the use to which it was put. In many cases, the occupier was also the owner, in which case you will find 'himself' written in the occupier's column, against the owner's name. The tithe survey does not go so far as the Valuation Office survey in stating the terms of the rent and describing the buildings. However, it can be very useful in giving some idea of the kind of holding a person had: whether he or she was simply a cottager, renting a house and garden on a small plot, or farmer of a large acreage.

Women

The majority of original apportionments list landowners and occupiers by their full first name and surname without the appellation 'Mr' or 'Mrs', except in the case of clerical or aristocratic titles. Thus, it is clear from the name whether the person was a woman, e.g. 'Mary Bell', rather than 'John Bell'. In altered apportionments, especially those of the first decades of the twentieth century, in many cases only the initial of the first name is given, but in the case of women, their marital status may be specified, e.g. 'spinster' or 'married woman'.

Other parishioners

Some tithe files contain information about the general population. The assistant commissioners' reports may comment on the type of occupation, social status and living conditions. The minutes of meetings held in the parish often record comments made by local residents about tithing customs in the area. In cases of dispute, witnesses were called to give evidence about title to land and tithe, and property boundaries.

Mapmakers, valuers and tithe officials

Two-thirds of the tithe maps in the National Archives bear the names of their makers; these names are listed alphabetically in Appendices 3 and 4 of Kain and Oliver, together with the names of the tithe districts which they mapped. Some of these men also undertook the valuation work required for tithe commutation, but in many cases this was undertaken separately by valuers and surveyors. The names of the latter can be found in the apportionment, at the end of the recital of the agreement or award. Reference to these men can sometimes be found, too, in the tithe files; in some cases, especially where there was a dispute, the valuer was required to make a report on his work. There may also be reference to the amount paid for valuers' and surveyors' work.

In some cases, the valuer was already acting as land agent to one or more of the landowners concerned. Appendix 1 of Kain and Oliver lists the names of assistant tithe commissioners and local tithe agents, together with the counties in which they worked. The name of the assistant tithe commissioner who officiated in a particular tithe district is given in the preamble to the apportionment, and his signature is often found on the map. An impression of his character may be gained by reading his reports, which may reveal his attitude towards the local population, where such terms as 'feckless', 'irresponsible' and 'indigent' may be written.

Another official who may be mentioned in the tithe files was the tithe collector, often a surveyor or valuer, who may have been required to report on the tithe collection over the previous ten years. Where these reports are found, they can give remarkable detail, and suggest a pattern of hardship and decline for farmers through the 1830s, with tithe collectors having to accept less than the figure they requested, owing to the poor state of farming. Such reports may go into the detail of individual owners and the circumstances of their tithe payments; perhaps that they were having a difficult time and could not pay the full amount, or even that they had absconded from the district without payment.

Figure 10 Decorative detail from the tithe map of Shevioch, Cornwall (IR 30/6/173), showing the names of the surveyors, Richard Eastcott and R. Frise of Devonport.

Information about places

The records of the tithe survey together can provide a great deal of information about a particular place. The map shows the layout of roads, fields and other features in the landscape. The apportionment usually gives statistics as to the area and state of cultivation of the lands in the tithe district; the extent of the land subject to tithes and of any lands exempt on various grounds from payment of tithes; and the area covered by commons, roads, wastes etc. Papers on the tithe file may amplify this: they may provide a useful overview of the place and any problems such as distance from water or roads; type of soil and farming, productivity levels, farming customs, industry, population. The assistant commissioner's report, where found, is especially likely to be useful, as it was required to describe the parish, and is often filled in at length. The report may contain information about local roads; about woodland management; and about access to local and wider markets. There may also be useful background information about other issues which tithe commutation raised such as boundary and title disputes. Such matters as the sale of glebe lands and the demolition of tithe barns may also be mentioned.

Fields and land use

The tithe apportionments are a wonderful source for field names. The majority of tithe plots were fields, and very often the field name is given in the apportionment. The plot number allows one to locate each named field on the map, which itself rarely bears this kind of information. The recording of field names is an especially useful feature of the tithe survey, since Ordnance Survey maps do not usually provide field names, although they do give the acreage of each field, also given in the tithe apportionment, which can help in finding the tithe plot on a modern map.

Orchards, hop fields and market gardens were carefully recorded, since they might be subject to an extra rentcharge because of their higher yield. Yet there is rarely any detail about other crops grown; land is simply differentiated between arable and pasture, in most cases – an important distinction since arable land was more valuable than pasture. The apportionment rarely mentions livestock, since the tithes on these were less valuable than those on crops. Some information on the type of livestock may be given in the tithe file.

The maps can also enable us to build up a picture of local agricultural practices, such as the persistence of open-field systems.

Field boundaries

Tithe maps depict field boundaries as they were just before the advent of widespread changes to the landscape. Boundary features such as hedgerows, fences, stiles, gates and hedgerow trees may be shown. Hedges may be drawn in such a way as to indicate ownership.

Landscape features

Tithe plots other than fields are also recorded in the apportionment. Woodland is often noted, since in some places tithe was payable on timber or, more commonly, on underwood. Woodland is often depicted on the maps by drawings of trees or colouring to differentiate it from farmland. Moorland and other areas of rough grazing were also noted, as they had a lower rateable value than average farmland. In coastal areas, cliffs, headlands and beaches may be shown. Features not subject to tithes may nevertheless be recorded: for instance, bodies of water, chalk pits, mines and quarries. The apportionment may also give details of non-titheable lands,

Figure 11 An unusually attractive watercolour, the tithe map of Boconnoc, Cornwall (IR 30/6/11), shows detail of a deer park, farms, and other features such as a 'pheasantry' (top left). The names of neighbouring parishes are shown along the parish boundaries.

which included: waste lands, glebe lands in the parson's occupation, lands which had not paid tithes from time immemorial, former monastic lands, Crown land, common land and public roads. Some maps give a relatively complete picture of the district, showing archaeological features; the village green or market square; burial grounds; canals and towpaths, railways with embankments and perhaps a viaduct; country houses complete with gardens, parks, stables and kennels. Many others are outline maps only, providing the bare necessities required to illustrate the apportionment.

Buildings

As stated earlier, it was not just farm land that was subject to tithes. Tithes could be payable in central urban areas as well as villages and agricultural communities. Although the tithe survey was not concerned with buildings as such, they are often shown on the maps, drawn in plan, and listed with names of owner and occupier in the apportionment. Inhabited buildings are usually shown in red on the maps, and other structures in grey: commonly, you will see a farmhouse in red, and the outbuildings in grey. Many maps show churches, chapels, inns, bakehouses, schools, smithies, mills and factories. Such features are rarely named on the maps (although churches are apparent from their cross shape in plan), but may be identified by using the map and apportionment together. The buildings most frequently identified in the apportionment are designated 'House and garden'; cottages are often noted. One may also find more unusual buildings, such as icehouses, dovecotes and lighthouses; the pagoda in Kew Gardens is clearly depicted on the Richmond tithe map. No further detail is given of the internal arrangement of buildings, as is sometimes seen in the field books of the 1910 Valuation Office survey. In some apportionments, buildings are listed separately, after the titheable lands.

Parish boundaries

Boundaries of parishes and townships are depicted on the tithe maps. There may be notes in the tithe files explaining the origins and peculiarities of local boundaries, and documenting the enquiries made before a decision on them was taken. In cases where it was necessary for the assistant tithe commissioners to define parish or township boundaries in order to establish who was entitled to receive tithes on a particular piece of land, you may find a Boundary Award in **TITH 1**. These proceedings were contemporary with the first Ordnance Survey exercise in defining parish boundaries; it may be useful to consult the Boundary Remark Books in **OS 26** and the Boundary Sketch Maps in **OS 27**.

Roads and paths

Roads were exempt from tithes, as they were not productive land, so their portrayal is incidental to the purpose of the tithe survey. However, roads are usually shown on tithe maps, where they bounded or crossed individual tithe areas. Only rarely is their status as public or private indicated with any certainty, although the general convention of colouring public roads in brown is often followed. On some tithe maps, roads are numbered, which means that they are referred to in the apportionment. There is an example in the Down St Mary case study, where a numbered plot is described as 'house, buildings and lane'. The extent of the lane is depicted on the map, and its owner named in the apportionment. Footpaths are not always shown on tithe maps, since they were not relevant for tithe purposes: they may be shown by annotation, or by single or double pecked lines. Where bridleways are shown, there is usually a text label alongside the line to indicate this. It is rare for rights of way to be unequivocally indicated on tithe maps, and no inferences should be drawn from the presence or absence of such information.

The tithe files may contain information about the condition of local roads, the existence of main roads and turnpikes. The maps sometimes show Roman roads, occupation roads, or toll gates. A few tithe maps of towns name individual streets.

Summary

The records produced by the Tithe Commission were just one product of the early Victorian administrative revolution. They are contemporary with the mid-century censuses of population, the beginnings of civil registration, Poor Law reform and the genesis of large-scale Ordnance Survey maps. Used in conjunction with other records of the period, the tithe survey can tell us much about a family and a locality at that time. Subsequent tithe records can provide later snapshots of the area, at intervals between the mid-nineteenth and mid-twentieth centuries.

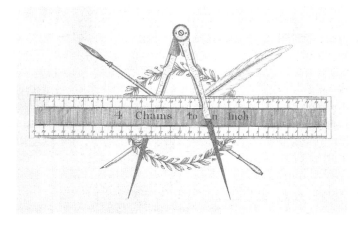

Figure 12 Decorative detail from the tithe map of Shevioch, Cornwall (IR 30/6/173), showing mapmakers' instruments.

3 The Valuation Office survey, 1910–15

Have you found an ancestor or property through the 1901 census? The Valuation Office survey, made a decade later, may help carry your research forward.

The Valuation Office records were made for tax administration following the 1910 Budget. They show the use and value of lands and buildings in Edwardian England and Wales. They provide information about more places than either the tithe or the National Farm surveys, and contain a wealth of detail about people and places immediately before the First World War.

Why was the survey carried out?

In the early years of the twentieth century, much of the land in Great Britain was still owned by a privileged few. Many people considered this to be a social injustice. Moreover, land often increased in value even though no capital outlay had been made by the landowner. In 1909, the Liberal Government, of which Lloyd George was Chancellor of the Exchequer (hence the survey is sometimes referred to as the Lloyd George survey), introduced a number of land clauses into the Budget, aimed at ensuring that private landowners should pay part of the increase in land values that was attributable not to their own labour and efforts for improvements but to expenditure by the State – for example in the provision of improved roads, drainage and other public services. However, the landed interest maintained great power in Parliament and these clauses were fiercely resisted. The Bill was rejected by the House of Lords, a 12-month struggle ensued, and it was not until after a general election that the Bill reached the statute book as the Finance (1909–1910) Act 1910 (hereafter called the 1910 Act).

The 1910 Act provided for the levying of a number of duties on land, the principal one being called increment value duty. This was to be levied at the rate of 20% on any increase in the site value of land between the time of its initial valuation as at 30 April 1909 and the occasion of its sale or other transfer, the grant of leases for more than 14 years, or the death of the owner. In the case of land held by corporate bodies, increment value duty was to be calculated every 15 years. Farmland was exempt if it had no greater value than its current agricultural market value. House-owners with land less than 50 acres in extent and worth less than £75 an acre were also exempt.

In order to obtain the 'datum line' (the basic valuation from which increases in value would be calculated), section 26(1) of the 1910 Act provided for a valuation to be made of the land of the United Kingdom as at 30 April 1909. This valuation was to

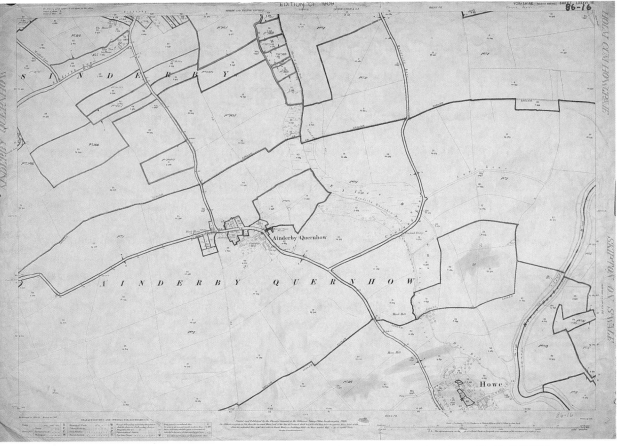

Figure 13 A Valuation Office map of Ainderby Quernhow, North Yorkshire (IR 134/4/457). The names of the relevant income tax parishes are written in the margins of the map. The numbers added in red ink are the hereditament numbers used to identify entries in the field books.

include *all* property, whether it was later to be considered exempt or not. It was anticipated that the valuation process, a 'New Domesday', would be of great future assistance to the business of central government, helping with a reform of the rating system and in cases of compulsory purchase.

Many landowners continued to oppose the Act's land clauses, and carried on their fight, mainly through the law courts where a number of test cases resulted in defeat for the government and challenged the whole basis of the valuation. The outbreak of the First World War interrupted the opposition to the land clauses, although the valuation process continued.

Increment value duty was repealed by the Finance Act 1920. The valuation survey had cost in excess of two million pounds, not a fraction of which was recovered by the government from payment of increment value duty. But this fiscal white elephant resulted in the creation of a detailed archive which provides a wealth of information about the population of Britain, their homes and workplaces, just before the immense social changes which followed the First World War.

How was the survey carried out?

The valuation was carried out by the Valuation Office of the Board of Inland Revenue. The Valuation Office had recently been set up to value property for the purposes of Estate Duty. In 1910, its establishment numbered only 61 people; in order to carry out the valuation required by the 1910 Act, this staff was greatly expanded, so that by July 1914, it numbered some 600 permanent personnel, with an additional 4,500 temporary employees.

To provide for the physical execution of the valuation, England and Wales were divided into 14 valuation divisions, which in turn were subdivided into 118 valuation districts. Within each valuation district, a number of so-called income tax parishes (ITPs) were created, and it was the income tax parish which constituted the basic administrative unit for the Valuation Office survey.

The valuation process began during the summer of 1910. As a first step, the Valuation Office created Valuation Books (sometimes known as 'Domesday Books'), which were the first major record of each unit of property to be valued (called an assessment or, more usually, a hereditament). From August, landowners country-wide were sent a form, Form 4-Land, which 'an owner of land or any person receiving rent in respect of land' was required to complete and return to the district valuation office. Instructions on how to fill in the form were included. The penalty for not returning the completed form was £50 (just over £3,000 in modern values). By the end of the year, approximately ten-and-a-half million forms had been sent out, all but a million of which had been returned.

The information from the returned Form 4-Land was transcribed into the valuer's field book, which was intended to become the final record of the valuation, and a physical inspection of all properties was now made. Maps were drawn up showing the location and extent of each property and plot of land to be valued. The inspection was a very time-consuming process. By 1912, the district valuation offices were running well behind the planned schedule, and instructions were issued to carry out certain aspects of the survey more quickly. In particular, farms (which until then had been recorded in great detail in the field books, often with plans showing all their buildings) were recorded more summarily.

The outbreak of the First World War, drawing off as it did many of the Valuation Office staff, put an additional strain on the valuation process, but the main work of the original valuation was completed by the autumn of 1915, only six months behind schedule.

Records of the Valuation Office survey

The principal series of records of the Valuation Office survey held by the National Archives are the **field books** and the **record maps**.

As described above, the information on each hereditament gained from the Forms 4-Land and by inspection in the field was recorded in the field books. The maps provide a graphic index to the field book entries.

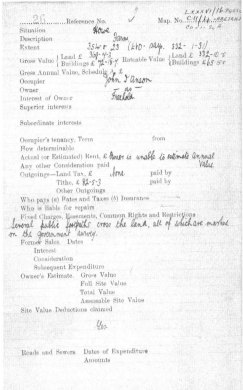

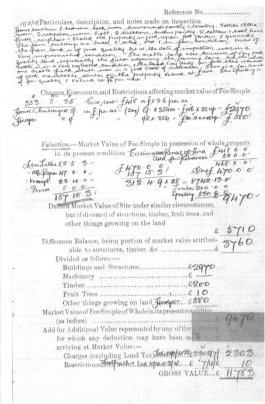

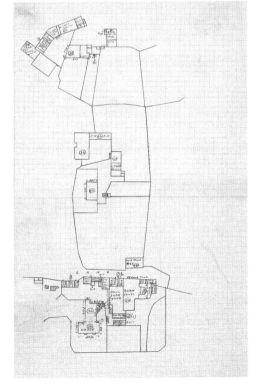

Figures 14a and 14b The first and second pages of the Valuation Office field book entry relating to Howe Farm in Ainderby Quernhow (IR 58/58527, no. 26).

Figure 14c The third page of the Valuation Office field book entry relating to plot 26 in Ainderby Quernhow includes a detailed plan on which all the farm buildings are named.

You will need to find the right map sheet to locate the property in which you are interested, then make a note of its hereditament number and identify the appropriate field book, in which you will find a description of the property. Without the hereditament number, it can be very difficult to locate the field book entry relating to a particular property, unless the property is in a very small parish which is listed separately rather than grouped with other parishes. Consequently, the first step in any search is usually to find the relevant map sheet.

The record maps

Although based on published Ordnance Survey maps, the unique value of these maps lies in the manuscript additions which provide a means of reference to the field books.
Two sets of maps were created in the course of the valuation exercise:

- **Working plans** were used by the valuers in the field during the actual survey. Many bear additional comments and other markings relating to the hereditaments, and notes about such matters as valuations, rights of way and property ownership. Many are annotated with references which are not pertinent to 1910 hereditaments but relate to the later business of the Valuation Office; some such annotations are as late in date as the 1970s. Most surviving working plans are in local record offices.

- **Record sheet plans** were marked up with the hereditament numbers and the boundaries of hereditaments. They were intended to be a permanent reference tool and record of the hereditaments, and therefore were kept in the district valuation offices and not taken into the field. Most are mounted on linen.

The maps held by the National Archives are mostly record sheet plans, but they do include some working plans. They make up a total of 51,652 producible pieces but are believed to number between 70,000 and 80,000 individual sheets. Many pieces consist of more than one sheet (identified as 'parts' in the catalogues); these are usually duplicates of the Ordnance Survey base map, but the information added in manuscript is likely to be different on every sheet. It may be necessary to examine all the sheets in a piece in order to obtain the required information.

What do the maps show?

The maps are printed Ordnance Survey sheets at various scales, to which the district valuation offices added, normally in red ink, the hereditament numbers – one number for each property or parcel of land.
Whenever possible, the Valuation Office used the largest scale and the most recent edition of Ordnance Survey mapping available. Irrespective of their Valuation Office content, these maps are a major resource of Ordnance Survey large-scale plans of the

late nineteenth and early twentieth centuries. The date range of the Ordnance Survey maps as printed is approximately 1880 to 1915. However, some of the maps at very large scales date from the mid-nineteenth century.

The most frequently used scale was 1:2500 (about 25 inches to the mile). However, the following scales were also used:

- 1:10,560 (6 inches to the mile) – for moorland and upland areas of low population density
- 1:1250 (about 50 inches to the mile) – for urban areas
- 1:1056 (60 inches to the mile: the so-called five-foot plans) – for London
- 1:528 (10 feet to the mile) – for towns and cities
- 1:500 (about 10 feet to the mile) – for towns and cities

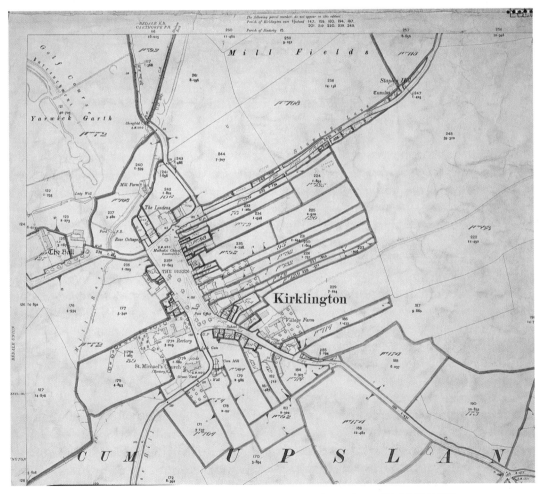

Figure 15 Another Valuation Office map of Ainderby Quernhow (IR 134/4/456). The hereditament numbers are identifiable in red ink. Notice that some pre-enclosure landscape remained even in the early twentieth century.

The printed six-inch maps show street names but not individual buildings. The 1:2500 maps show street names, individual fields (with acreage) and buildings. The cartographic information on the 1:1250 sheets is identical to that on the 1:2500 survey, as the former are purely a photographic enlargement of the latter. The increased scale, however, may make certain details clearer. The very large-scale maps (1:500 and 1:528) were not derived from existing maps but were made quite separately and contain a great deal of additional detail, including exact block plans of buildings, the names of detached houses, the layout of gardens (paths, trees, ponds and greenhouses are all shown), the width of street pavements, and even the positions of individual lamp-posts, pillar boxes and watering-troughs.

The Valuation Office surveyors added information about each unit of property to the maps. The hereditament number for each property was written on the map, normally in red ink, one number for each property or parcel of land. Occasionally the number is in black ink; in such cases care must be taken not to confuse the Valuation Office hereditament number with the Ordnance Survey land parcel number or acreage figure – these are normally printed in the centre of each field. The hereditament number should be used to identify the related entry in the field book (see p. 55).

The extent of each hereditament is usually shown by a colour wash along the boundaries, often in pink or green. On some maps, all such boundaries are shown in the same colour, on others each property boundary is in a different colour to aid differentiation. Sometimes the whole of each area of valuation is filled in with coloured wash. However, this practice was not universal, and the district valuation offices often used differing colours.

Separate parts of a hereditament divided by a feature such as a road or a stream are usually shown joined together by a brace (normally in red ink). This is the same type of brace as used by the Ordnance Survey on its printed maps to link split parcels of land. Sometimes the Valuation Office used half-braces to emphasize the boundaries of part hereditaments.

Where several detached parcels of land had a common owner and formed a single hereditament, each of these is shown on the map as a 'Part' or 'Pt.', e.g. 'Pt 72' in Figure 15. Sometimes the number of parts involved is given on the map (often shown as a figure in brackets after the hereditament and part number). Often, the field books provide a schedule of the parts, using the Ordnance Survey parcel numbers and acreage figures as references. In the case of a large estate, the various parts of a hereditament may well extend over several map sheets.

If the property in which you are interested is not marked with a hereditament number on the map you are consulting, it may be that the Valuation Office used a map at a larger scale for that area and that you will need to seek the relevant 1:1250 or 1:500 sheet. This is particularly likely in the case of urban areas.

Many maps also show the boundaries of income tax parishes. Such boundaries are often marked in yellow. Sometimes the names of income tax parishes are written or stamped (usually in red) in the margins of the map. Occasionally, the name of the income tax parish is written in with the hereditament number. This information may be given in abbreviated form on the map; for example, maps of the Forest of Dean identify certain hereditaments as being in West Dean by inserting the letters W.D. in front of the hereditament number. There is not usually any key to the meaning of such abbreviations; reference to local place names will often decipher them. It can be vital to have the name of the income tax parish when you are seeking a field book entry.

How are the maps arranged?

The Valuation Office record sheet plans are arranged according to the Valuation Office regions as they were in 1988 when the maps were transferred to the Public Record Office. Maps from each region were placed in a separate record series as follows:

IR 121	London region
IR 124	South East region
IR 125	Wessex region
IR 126	Central region
IR 127	East Anglia region
IR 128	Western region
IR 129	West Midland region
IR 130	East Midland region
IR 131	Welsh region
IR 132	Liverpool region
IR 133	Manchester region
IR 134	Yorkshire region
IR 135	Northern region

Each region was divided administratively into a number of districts, and the maps relating to each district (again, as they were in 1988) were placed in a separate sub-series, as follows.

List of Valuation Office districts

London region	IR 121	Wessex region	IR 125
Merton	IR 121/1	Bournemouth	IR 125/1
Barking	IR 121/2	Dorset County West	IR 125/2
Barnet	IR 121/3	Guildford	IR 125/3
Bexley & Greenwich	IR 121/4	N E Hampshire	IR 125/4
Bromley	IR 121/5	North Surrey	IR 125/5
Camden	IR 121/6	Portsmouth	IR 125/6
City of London	IR 121/7	(no surviving records)	
Croydon	IR 121/8	Salisbury	IR 125/7
Ealing	IR 121/9	Solent	IR 125/8
Enfield	IR 121/10	Solent (IOW)	IR 125/9
Hammersmith & Fulham	IR 121/11	Southampton	IR 125/10
Harrow (Hillingdon)	IR 121/12	(no surviving records)	
Hounslow	IR 121/13	Wiltshire North	IR 125/11
Islington	IR 121/14		
Kensington & Chelsea	IR 121/15	Western region	IR 128
Lambeth	IR 121/16		
Redbridge	IR 121/17	Barnstaple	IR 128/1
Richmond-upon-Thames	IR 121/18	Bath	IR 128/2
Southwark	IR 121/19	Bristol	IR 128/3
Tower Hamlets	IR 121/20	Cheltenham	IR 128/4
Westminster 1	IR 121/21	Cornwall	IR 128/5
Westminster 2	IR 121/22	Exeter	IR 128/6
		Gloucester	IR 128/7
		Plymouth	IR 128/8
South Eastern region	IR 124	Somerset	IR 128/9
		Torbay	IR 128/10
Brighton	IR 124/1		
Canterbury	IR 124/2	Welsh region	IR 131
Canterbury (Maidstone)	IR 124/3		
Eastbourne	IR 124/4	Abergavenny	IR 131/1
East Kent	IR 124/5	Bangor	IR 131/2
Medway	IR 124/6	Bangor (Colwyn Bay)	IR 131/3
Reigate	IR 124/7	Cardiff	IR 131/4
Tunbridge Wells	IR 124/8	Dyfed	IR 131/5
Worthing	IR 124/9	Merthyr Tydfil	IR 131/6
		Newport	IR 131/7
		Pontypridd	IR 131/8
		Swansea	IR 131/9
		Wrexham	IR 131/10
		Wrexham (Welshpool)	IR 131/11

List of Valuation Office districts

Northern region	IR 135	Yorkshire region	IR 134
Carlisle	IR 135/1	Bradford	IR 134/1
Cleveland	IR 135/2	Calderdale	IR 134/2
Darlington	IR 135/3	Doncaster	IR 134/3
Durham	IR 135/4	Harrogate	IR 134/4
Newcastle	IR 135/5	Hull	IR 134/5
Newcastle (Tyneside)	IR 135/6	Kirklees	IR 134/6
Northumberland	IR 135/7	Leeds	IR 134/7
South Lakeland	IR 135/8	Sheffield	IR 134/8
Sunderland	IR 135/9	Wakefield	IR 134/9
		York	IR 134/10
Liverpool region	IR 132	Manchester region	IR 133
Chester	IR 132/1	Bolton	IR 133/1
East Cheshire	IR 132/2	East Lancashire	IR 133/2
Liverpool	IR 132/3	Lancaster	IR 133/3
Shropshire	IR 132/4	Manchester	IR 133/4
Stafford	IR 132/5	Preston	IR 133/5
Stoke-on-Trent	IR 132/6	Rochdale	IR 133/6
Warrington	IR 132/7	Salford	IR 133/7
Wigan	IR 132/8	Stockport	IR 133/8
West Midland region	IR 129	East Midland region	IR 130
Birmingham	IR 129/1	Boston	IR 130/1
Coventry	IR 129/2	Derby	IR 130/2
Hereford & Worcester	IR 129/3	Grimsby	IR 130/3
Kidderminster	IR 129/4	Leicester	IR 130/4
Lichfield	IR 129/5	Lincoln	IR 130/5
Sandwell	IR 129/6	Loughborough	IR 130/6
Walsall	IR 129/7	Mansfield	IR 130/7
Warwick	IR 129/8	Matlock	IR 130/8
Wolverhampton	IR 129/9	Nottingham	IR 130/9
Central region	IR 126	East Anglia region	IR 127
Aylesbury	IR 126/1	Basildon	IR 127/1
Bedfordshire	IR 126/2	(few surviving records)	
East Berkshire	IR 126/3	Cambridge	IR 127/2
Hertfordshire North	IR 126/4	Chelmsford	IR 127/3
Northampton	IR 126/5	Colchester	IR 127/4
Oxford	IR 126/6	Ipswich	IR 127/5
Reading	IR 126/7	Norwich	IR 127/6
St Albans	IR 126/8	Peterborough	IR 127/7
South Buckinghamshire	IR 126/9	Peterborough (King's Lynn)	IR 127/8
Watford	IR 126/10	St Edmundsbury	IR 127/9

Within each sub-series, the maps are listed first by county, then by scale and then by Ordnance Survey sheet number.

The following may help you to identify the most likely record series in which to find maps of the area you are seeking:

List of Valuation Office maps based on Ordnance Survey County Series

County	Scale	Reference
Anglesey	1:2500	IR 131/2
	1:1250	IR 131/2
Bedfordshire	1:2500	IR 126/2, IR 126/4, IR 127/7
	1:1250	IR 126/2
Berkshire	1:2500	IR 126/3, IR 126/6, IR 126/7
	1:1250	IR 126/7
Brecknockshire	1:2500	IR 131/1, IR 131/6, IR 131/8
	1:1250	IR 131/1, IR 131/6, IR 131/8
	1:10,560	IR 131/1
Buckinghamshire	1:2500	IR 126/1, IR 126/2, IR 126/3, IR 126/9
	1:1250	IR 126/1, IR 126/2, IR 126/3, IR 126/9
Cambridgeshire	1:2500	IR 127/2, IR 127/4, IR 127/7,
	1:1250	IR 127/2, IR 127/7, IR 127/9
Cardiganshire	1:2500	IR 131/5
	1:1250	IR 131/5
Carmarthenshire	1:2500	IR 131/5, IR 131/9
	1:1250	IR 131/5, IR 131/9
Carnarvonshire	1:10,560	IR 131/3
	1:2500	IR 131/2, IR 131/3
	1:1250	IR 131/2, IR 131/3
Cheshire	1:10,560	IR 133/8
	1:2500	IR 130/8, IR 132/1, IR 132/2, IR 132/7, IR 133/4, IR 133/7, IR 133/8
	1:1250	IR 132/1, IR 132/2, IR 133/7

List of Valuation Office maps based on Ordnance Survey County Series

County	Scale	Reference
Cornwall	1:2500	IR 128/5
Cumberland	1:10,560	IR 135/1
	1:2500	IR 135/1, IR 135/8
	1:1250	IR 135/1, IR 135/8
Denbighshire	1:10,560	IR 131/3
	1:2500	IR 131/3, IR 131/10
	1:1250	IR 131/3, IR 131/10
Derbyshire	1:2500	IR 130/2, IR 130/8, IR 134/3, IR 134/8
	1:1250	IR 130/2, IR 130/8, IR 134/8
Devon	1:2500	IR 128/1, IR 128/5, IR 128/6, IR 128/8, IR 128/9, IR 128/10
	1:1250	IR 128/1, IR 128/6, IR 128/8, IR 128/10
Dorset	1:2500	IR 125/1, IR 125/2, IR 128/6
	1:1250	IR 125/1, IR 125/2
Durham	1:10,560	IR 135/3, IR 135/4
	1:2500	IR 135/2, IR 135/3, IR 135/4, IR 135/5, IR 135/9
	1:1250	IR 135/2, IR 135/3, IR 135/4, IR 135/9
Essex	1:2500	IR 121/2, IR 121/17, IR 121/20, IR 127/1, IR 127/3, IR 127/4
	1:1250	IR 121/2, IR 121/17, IR 127/1, IR 127/3, IR 127/4
Flintshire	1:2500	IR 131/3, IR 131/10
	1:1250	IR 131/10
Glamorganshire	1:2500	IR 131/4, IR 131/6, IR 131/8, IR 131/9
	1:1250	IR 131/4, IR 131/6, IR 131/8, IR 131/9
Gloucestershire	1:2500	IR 128/2, IR 128/3, IR 128/4, IR 128/7, IR 129/8
	1:1250	IR 128/2, IR 128/3

List of Valuation Office maps based on Ordnance Survey County Series

County	Scale	Reference
Hampshire	1:10,560	IR 125/9
	1:2500	IR 125/1, IR 125/4, IR 125/7, IR 125/8, IR 125/9
	1:1250	IR 125/1, IR 125/4
Herefordshire	1:2500	IR 129/3, IR 131/1
	1:1250	IR 129/3
Hertfordshire	1:2500	IR 121/3, IR 126/2, IR 126/4, IR 126/8, IR 126/10, IR 127/3
	1:1250	IR 121/3, IR 126/8, IR 126/10
Huntingdonshire	1:2500	IR 127/7
	1:1250	IR 127/7
Kent	1:2500	IR 121/4, IR 121/5, IR 124/2, IR 124/3, IR 124/5, IR 124/6, IR 124/8
	1:1250	IR 124/2, IR 124/3, IR 124/5, IR 124/8
Lancashire	1:10,560	IR 135/8
	1:2500	IR 132/3, IR 132/7, IR 132/8, IR 133/1, IR 133/2, IR 133/3, IR 133/4, IR 133/5, IR 133/6, IR 133/7, IR 133/8, IR 135/8
	1:1250	IR 132/3, IR 132/7, IR 132/8, IR 133/1, IR 133/2, IR 133/3, IR 133/4, IR 133/5, IR 133/6, IR 133/7, IR 135/8
Leicestershire	1:2500	IR 130/4, IR 130/6
	1:1250	IR 130/4, IR 130/6
Lincolnshire	1:2500	IR 130/1, IR 130/3, IR 130/5, IR 134/5
	1:1250	IR 130/1, IR 130/3, IR 130/5, IR 134/5
London	1:2500	IR 121/5, IR 121/20
	1:1250	IR 121/17, IR 121/20
Merionethshire	1:2500	IR 131/2, IR 131/10
	1:1250	IR 131/2, IR 131/10
Middlesex	1:2500	IR 121/3, IR 121/9, IR 121/10, IR 121/11, IR 121/12, IR 121/13, IR 121/18, IR 126/10
	1:1250	IR 121/10

List of Valuation Office maps based on Ordnance Survey County Series

County	Scale	Reference
Monmouthshire	1:2500	IR 131/1, IR 131/4, IR 131/6, IR 131/7
	1:1250	IR 131/1, IR 131/6, IR 131/7
Montgomeryshire	1:2500	IR 131/11
Norfolk	1:2500	IR 127/6, IR 127/7, IR 127/8, IR 127/9
	1:1250	IR 127/6, IR 127/8
Northamptonshire	1:2500	IR 126/5, IR 127/7, IR 130/4
	1:1250	IR 126/5, IR 127/7
Northumberland	1:10,560	IR 135/7
	1:2500	IR 135/5, IR 135/6, IR 135/7
	1:1250	IR 135/7
Nottinghamshire	1:2500	IR 130/5, IR 130/7, IR 130/9, IR 134/3
	1:1250	IR 130/7, IR 130/9
Oxfordshire	1:2500	IR 126/1, IR 126/6
	1:1250	IR 126/6
Pembrokeshire	1:2500	IR 131/5
	1:1250	IR 131/5
Radnorshire	1:2500	IR 131/1
	1:1250	IR 131/1
Rutland	1:2500	IR 130/5, IR 130/6
	1:1250	IR 130/6
Shropshire	1:2500	IR 131/1, IR 132/4
	1:1250	IR 132/4
Somerset	1:2500	IR 128/1, IR 128/2, IR 128/3, IR 128/9
	1:1250	IR 128/1, IR 128/2, IR 128/3, IR 128/9
Staffordshire	1:2500	IR 129/4, IR 129/5, IR 129/6, IR 129/7, IR 129/9, IR 132/5, IR 132/6
	1:1250	IR 129/1, IR 129/4, IR 129/5, IR 129/6, IR 129/7, IR 129/9, IR 132/5, IR 132/6
Suffolk	1:2500	IR 127/5, IR 127/6, IR 127/9
	1:1250	IR 127/5, IR 127/9

List of Valuation Office maps based on Ordnance Survey County Series

County	Scale	Reference
Surrey	1:2500	IR 121/1, IR 121/8, IR 121/18, IR 124/7, IR 125/3, IR 125/5
	1:1250	IR 121/1, IR 121/18, IR 124/7, IR 125/3, IR 125/5
Sussex	1:10,560	IR 124/1
	1:2500	IR 124/1, IR 124/4, IR 124/8, IR 124/9
	1:1250	IR 124/1, IR 124/9
Warwickshire	1:2500	IR 129/2, IR 129/5, IR 129/6, IR 129/7, IR 129/8
	1:1250	IR 129/1, IR 129/2, IR 129/8
Westmorland	1:10,560	IR 135/1
	1:2500	IR 135/1, IR 135/8
	1:1250	IR 135/1, IR 135/8
Wiltshire	1:2500	IR 125/7, IR 125/11, IR 128/2
	1:1250	IR 125/7, IR 125/11
Worcestershire	1:2500	IR 129/3, IR 129/4, IR 129/6, IR 129/8
	1:1250	IR 129/1, IR 129/3, IR 129/4, IR 129/6
Yorkshire: East Riding	1:2500	IR 134/5, IR 134/10
	1:1250	IR 134/5
Yorkshire: North Riding	1:10,560	IR 134/10, IR 135/8
	1:2500	IR 134/4, IR 134/10, IR 135/2, IR 135/3
	1:1250	IR 134/4, IR 134/10, IR 135/2
Yorkshire: West Riding	1:10,560	IR 133/2, IR 134/1, IR 134/2, IR 135/8
	1:2500	IR 133/2, IR 133/6, IR 134/1, IR 134/2, IR 134/3, IR 134/4, IR 134/5, IR 134/6, IR 134/7, IR 134/8, IR 134/9, IR 134/10, IR 135/8
	1:1250	IR 133/2, IR 134/1, IR 134/2, IR 134/3, IR 134/4, IR 134/6, IR 134/7, IR 134/8, IR 134/9, IR 134/10, IR 135/8

It is important to remember that the Valuation Office used large-scale maps whenever possible. So if the area you are seeking was in a town, it is always worth checking whether there are maps at a larger scale; many quite small towns were mapped at scales as large as 1:500 (about 10 feet to a mile). The following is a list of the towns represented at five feet to one mile or larger.

List of Valuation Office maps based on Ordnance Survey large-scale town plans

Place	Reference	Place	Reference
Aberystwyth	IR 131/5	Ashby de la Zouch	IR 130/6
Alnwick	IR 135/7		
Barnsley	IR 134/9	Bradford	IR 134/1
Barnstaple	IR 128/1	Bradford-on-Avon	IR 125/7
Bath	IR 128/2	Bridgnorth	IR 134/4
Batley	IR 134/6	Bridgwater	IR 128/9
Beccles	IR 127/5	Bridlington	IR 134/5
Berwick-upon-Tweed	IR 135/7	Brighouse	IR 134/2
Beverley	IR 134/5	Bristol	IR 128/3
Bideford	IR 128/1	Bromsgrove	IR 129/4
Bingley	IR 134/1	Buckingham	IR 126/1
Birmingham	IR 129/1, IR 29/6	Bury St Edmunds	IR 127/9
		Burton upon Trent	IR 129/5
Birstal	IR 134/6		
Cardiff	IR 131/4	Congleton	IR 132/2
Carmarthen	IR 131/5	Crediton	IR 128/1
Castleford	IR 134/9	Crewe	IR 132/2
Chelmsford	IR 127/3	Crewkerne	IR 128/9
Cleckheaton	IR 134/6		
Derby	IR 130/2	Doncaster	IR 134/3
Devizes	IR 125/11	Droitwich	IR 129/3
Dewsbury	IR 134/6	Dudley	IR 129/4
Elland	IR 134/2	Exeter	IR 128/6
Evesham	IR 129/3		
Farsley	IR 134/1, IR 134/7	Frome	IR 128/9
Gainsborough	IR 130/5	Great Driffield	IR 134/5
Garston	IR 132/3	Great Malvern	IR 129/3
Gateshead	IR 135/6, IR 135/9	Grimsby	IR 130/3
Goole	IR 134/5		

List of Valuation Office maps based on Ordnance Survey large-scale town plans

Place	Reference	Place	Reference
Halifax	IR 134/2	Heywood	IR 133/6
Harrogate	IR 134/4	Hinkley	IR 130/6
Hebden Bridge	IR 134/2	Horncastle	IR 130/1
Heckmondwike	IR 134/6	Huddersfield	IR 134/6
Hereford	IR 129/3	Hull	IR 134/5
Idle	IR 134/1	Ilkley	IR 134/1
Ilfracombe	IR 128/1	Ipswich	IR 127/5
Jarrow	IR 135/5	Kingston upon Hull	IR 134/5
		Knottingley	IR 134/9
Keighley	IR 134/1		
Kidderminster	IR 129/4		
King's Lynn	IR 127/8		
Leamington Spa	IR 129/8	London	IR 121/1,
Leeds	IR 134/7		IR 121/3–
Leicester	IR 130/4		IR 121/7,
Leominster	IR 129/3		IR 121/9–
Liverpool	IR 132/3		IR 121/11,
Loughborough	IR 130/6		IR 121/13–
Louth	IR 130/1		IR 121/22
Lowestoft	IR 127/5		
Ludlow	IR 132/4		
Manchester	IR 133/6	Middleton	IR 133/6
Melton Mowbray	IR 130/6	Mirfield	IR 134/6
Middlesbrough	IR 135/2	Morpeth	IR 135/7
Nantwich	IR 132/2	New Malton	IR 134/10
Newcastle upon Tyne	IR 135/5,	North Shields	IR 135/5
	IR 135/6,	Nottingham	IR 130/9
	IR 135/9		
Oldbury	IR 129/6	Otley	IR 134/4,
Oldham	IR 133/6		IR 134/7
Oswestry	IR 132/4	Oxford	IR 126/6
Plymouth	IR 128/8	Preston	IR 133/5
Pontefract	IR 134/9	Pudsey	IR 134/1,
			IR 134/7
Ravensthorpe	IR 134/6	Rochdale	IR 133/6
Redditch	IR 129/3	Rotherham	IR 134/3,
Richmond (Yorkshire)	IR 134/4		IR 134/8
		Royton	IR 133/6

List of Valuation Office maps based on Ordnance Survey large-scale town plans

Place	Reference	Place	Reference
Salford	IR 133/4	Southport	IR 132/3
Salisbury	IR 125/7	South Shields	IR 135/5
Saltaire	IR 134/1	Sowerby Bridge	IR 134/2
Scarborough	IR 134/10	Stanningley	IR 134/1,
Selby	IR 134/10		IR 134/7
Sheffield	IR 134/8	Stockton-on-Tees	IR 135/2
Shepton Mallet	IR 128/9	Stourbridge	IR 129/4
Shipley	IR 134/1	Stowmarket	IR 127/5
Shrewsbury	IR 132/4	Stratford-upon-Avon	IR 129/8
Skipton	IR 134/4	Sudbury	IR 127/9
Taunton	IR 128/9	Totnes	IR 128/10
Thetford	IR 127/9	Trowbridge	IR 125/7
Tiverton	IR 128/1	Tynemouth	IR 135/5
Todmorden	IR 134/2	Tyneside	IR 135/6
Torquay	IR 128/10		
Wakefield	IR 134/9	West Bromwich	IR 129/6
Walsall	IR 129/7	Whitby	IR 134/10
Wallsend	IR 135/5	Whitchurch	IR 132/4
Warminster	IR 125/7	Whitehaven	IR 135/8
Warwick	IR 129/8	Withington	IR 133/4
Wednesbury	IR 129/6	Woodbridge	IR 127/5
Wellington	IR 128/9	Worcester	IR 129/3
Yeovil	IR 128/9	York	IR 134/10

It is also important to bear in mind that the boundaries of the Valuation Office regions and districts, and indeed of certain counties, have altered since the time of the 1910–1915 survey. This can sometimes cause difficulty in identifying the required map sheet, and a measure of trial and error, together with some perseverance, may be necessary.

How to find and use the record maps

First obtain your Ordnance Survey map sheet number (see Chapter 5: **How to find an Ordnance Survey sheet number**).

Once you know the Ordnance Survey sheet number for the area in which you are interested, you can get the document reference for a map in advance of your visit, by using the search facility on the online catalogue from the National Archives website. Because the county names have not been entered into the online catalogue at the same level as the sheet numbers, it is necessary to make a search in two stages and collate the results to arrive at the document ordering reference.

So if, for example, you are looking for Ordnance Survey 1:2500 sheet Hertfordshire XIX.4, the search should proceed along the following lines:

1. Identify the record series containing maps of Hertfordshire. The easiest way to do this is to make an online search using 'Hertfordshire' as a search term, 1910 as the date and limiting the search to 'IR'. This will give the following result:

IR 121/3	Board of Inland Revenue: Valuation Office: Finance Act 1910, Record Sheet Plans: London Region: Barnet District	c1910
IR 126/2	Board of Inland Revenue: Valuation Office: Finance Act 1910, Record Sheet Plans: Central Region: Bedfordshire District	c1910
IR 126/4	Board of Inland Revenue: Valuation Office: Finance Act 1910, Record Sheet Plans: Central Region: Hertfordshire North District	c1910
IR 126/8	Board of Inland Revenue: Valuation Office: Finance Act 1910, Record Sheet Plans: Central Region: St Albans District	c1910
IR 126/10	Board of Inland Revenue: Valuation Office: Finance Act 1910, Record Sheet Plans: Central Region: Watford District	c1910

2. Specify your sheet number (but not county name) in the search field, and type the lettercode IR in the reference field. This will yield 36 results, of which only the following relates to any of the record series identified above:

IR 126/4/152	OS Sheet Reference: XIX 4

3. Click on the right-hand element shown above to obtain a full description of the document.

4. Click on the 'Context' button to confirm which county the sheet relates to. In this case, the reference **IR 126/4/152** is indeed Hertfordshire XIX.4.

This is often also the easiest way to get a document reference during your visit, via the computer terminals in the reading rooms.

If you prefer, you can also get the reference by using the paper series lists at the National Archives. Make a note of the number in the column to the left of the Ordnance Survey sheet number you require; this is the piece number.

When looking for a map of an area in a 'new county' created in 1974, search under the name of the county in which the place lay in the early twentieth century. A reference map showing the alterations to county boundaries in 1974 is available in the Map and Large Document Reading Room. If you cannot find a record map for an area near the borders of one county, it may be worth looking under the adjacent county.

Many of the maps are in a poor state of repair and should be handled with care. The National Archives Conservation Department repairs a considerable number of Valuation Office maps each year, but the numbers involved are huge and it will be many years before the work can be completed. If you find a map which is badly torn or which is peeling away from the linen backing, please inform a member of staff so that the map can be noted for conservation treatment.

If you already have a hereditament number from another source and are seeking the relevant map, note that the field books often give the relevant Ordnance Survey sheet number against the hereditament number on the first page of the entry. Such a sheet number may be immediately followed by a letter of the alphabet; these letters indicated the general area of the map sheet on which the particular property is shown. Each sheet was mentally divided into 16 sections – four from left to right and four from top to bottom (see Figure 16). An easy way to remember which letters were used is to exclude those letters which were used as Roman numerals (C, D, I, L and M and X).

The field books

The information derived from the landowners and from the surveyors was written up into small (10 inches by 6 inches and 1 inch thick), specially printed volumes known as field books. They number about 95,000. They are all in the record series **IR 58**. Each field book contains space for 100 entries, each entry relating to a single hereditament. The field books are arranged in alphabetical order of valuation district and, within districts, by income tax parish. It is believed that this order reflects the arrangement of district valuation offices when increment value duty was repealed in 1920; it does not necessarily correspond to the arrangement within which the record maps are now kept.

An income tax parish (ITP) might consist of a single civil parish, only part of a civil parish, or a number of neighbouring civil parishes. In the latter case, the ITP usually took the name of the first place in an alphabetical list of the constituent parishes. For example, the ITP headed by the civil parish of Alton in Hampshire also contained the parishes of Binstead, Chawton, Dockenfield, Farringdon, Newton Valence, Shalden and East Tisted. Only the name Alton is given in the **IR 58** catalogue; the hereditaments in the other parishes will be found in the Alton field books, but are not separately shown in the catalogue.

It can sometimes be difficult to establish the name of the income tax parish in which a particular place lay. You may find the name of an ITP by one of the following means:

1. Look at the relevant map: the name may be written or stamped in the margin or added in manuscript after the hereditament number.
2. Look up your place in the Board of Inland Revenue's *Alphabetical List of Parishes and Places in England and Wales* (on the open shelves in the Map and Large Document Reading Room). This volume may provide the name of the income tax parish in which your place was included in the column headed, 'United with or included in'. However, as the volume is dated 1897 and there were many alterations to the composition of income tax parishes over the years, the correct information will not be found in every case.

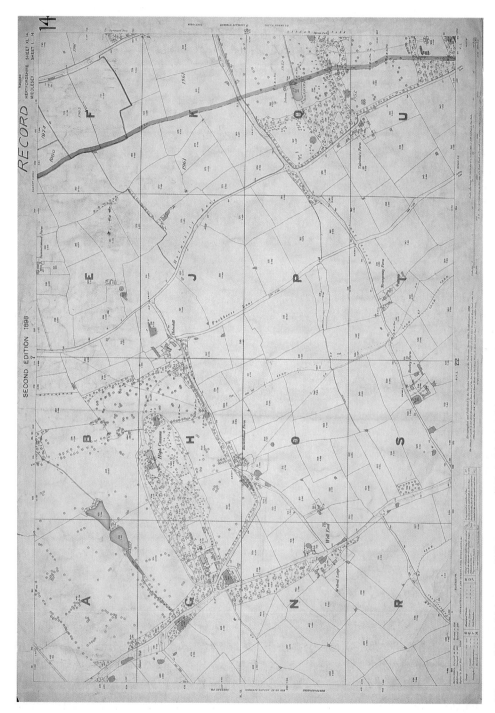

Figure 16 A Valuation Office map of Enfield, Middlesex, marked in manuscript to show the lettered squares representing different areas of the map as used in the field books to indicate the approximate position of a plot on a map sheet (IR 121/10/9).

Local knowledge can often be the best guide. Geraldine discovered that the entries relating to Boreham Wood, where her parents lived, were in the field books for Aldenham ITP. Boreham Wood was only a tiny hamlet in 1910, but is now much bigger than Aldenham. By referring to the **IR 58** catalogue, you will be able to discard any ITP name for which the highest hereditament number listed is lower than the hereditament number you are seeking. This is likely to involve a certain amount of trial and error.

The best source for the composition of an ITP is the appropriate Valuation Book (see p. 64).

Having obtained the name of the ITP and the hereditament number, you need to look at the online catalogue or the paper series catalogue for **IR 58** in order to obtain the document reference for the relevant field book. It may require some persistence to establish which is the correct field book for the area in which you are interested.

Bear in mind that records do not survive for all places. Here is a list of areas for which some or all of the maps and/or field books are known not to survive:

Basildon – many records destroyed by a fire in the District Valuation Office
Birkenhead and most of the Wirral – believed to have been destroyed by enemy action during the Second World War
Chelmsford – many records for the town and surrounding area do not survive; it is believed that they may have been in the Basildon office at the time of the fire, but this is not certain
Chichester – destroyed by enemy action during the Second World War
Coventry – lost in the Second World War
Liverpool – believed to have been destroyed by enemy action during the Second World War
Portsmouth – destroyed by enemy action during the Second World War (the series **IR 125/6** was allocated even though no maps survive)
Southampton – destroyed by enemy action during the Second World War (the series **IR 125/10** was allocated even though no maps survive)
Winchester – destroyed by enemy action during the Second World War.

There may be other gaps – please notify National Archives staff if you are aware of any others.

What do the field books show?

The principal function of the field books was to record the assessable site value on the basis of which increment value duty was to be calculated. Four sets of valuation figures are given for each hereditament. These were arrived at after a series of complicated calculations, which can be simplified as follows:

Gross Value – the amount which the land might be expected to make on the open market, free of any encumbrances

Full Site Value – the amount which remained after deducting the value of the buildings from the gross value of the land

Total Value – the gross value, with deductions made for fixed charges, rights of way, and rights of common

Assessable Site Value – the total value, with the same deduction made to arrive at the full site value from the gross value, but with additional deductions for work and expenditure made by the owner to improve the land.

It was on the assessable site value that increment value duty was payable.

There is a four-page entry for each hereditament. The amount of information given varies considerably, but you might hope to find the full street address of the property; an interior and exterior description (including the number and use of rooms and the state of repair, and sometimes a detailed plan); the name of the owner and of the occupier; the date of construction and of any previous sales, and the valuation figures, as well as a schedule of all neighbouring lands owned. Farms are often described at length. Sometimes public buildings, such as town halls, schools, churches and cathedrals are recorded in a detail that seems far beyond the actual requirements of the survey. Entries relating to public buildings and those relating to locations not in individual ownership, such as commons, parks, historic sites, etc., are often grouped together at the end of a parish. In the urban landscape, descriptions of factories, gas works, banks, hotels and other significant buildings can be obtained. Sometimes the existence of public rights of way over the land is indicated in the valuation deductions column, and occasionally these rights of way are described, with the Ordnance Survey parcel numbers of the fields through which they pass.

The field books often did not contain enough space to include all the details of the hereditaments which made up large properties and estates. For such cases, the Valuation Office created special files, to which the field books refer, often in the form 'description filed': it is not thought that any such files have survived. The practice of making the major record of hereditaments outside the field book was carried out by certain valuation offices regardless of the size of the properties and land involved. For such properties, the sparse details in the field books can sometimes be supplemented by the Valuation Books and Forms 37-Land (see pp. 64, 66).

What kind of information can the Valuation Office survey provide for family and local historians?

There is a wealth of detail in the records, although variable from area to area and between different surveyors. The usefulness of the information for family history varies from case to case: there is seldom detailed information about individuals or about relationships between people, but there can be quite a lot about homes, living conditions and the local environment. Local historians will find these records to be a rich source of information about buildings, land use and patterns of land-ownership.

People

The names and addresses of owners are given, where different from the occupier, on the first page of the field book entry. Very occasionally, one name is crossed out and another entered, reflecting the fact that the property had changed ownership (as shown in the Down St Mary case). There is rarely any extra information about the owner or the occupier, but a glance through the other entries for the same area will show if other holdings were owned by the same person. You may find owners described as 'the executors of the deceased's estate'; this can be particularly useful in cases where the entries are dated. Large landowners might own a number of properties in the parish. This was the case with the Duke of Devonshire at Chatsworth, who owned much of the surrounding land; there are separate field book entries for the kitchen gardens and home farm as well as for Chatsworth House itself, with its 79 bedrooms, 24 reception rooms and 12 halls. The valuer doubled his final valuation of this property, on the grounds of 'historic interest', which made the property even more valuable than it would otherwise have been.

Information is given about tenure and rents and about who paid the rates, land tax, tithes (i.e. tithe rentcharge) and insurance, and who was responsible for meeting the cost of repairs. Such details can be used in conjunction with information from other sources about the occupation and probable income of the occupier and so build up a

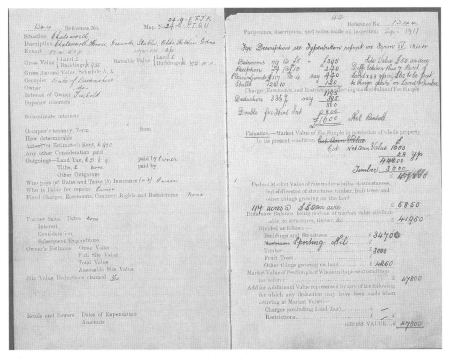

Figure 17 The Valuation Office field book entry relating to Chatsworth House in Derbyshire shows that the valuer doubled the increment value duty to be paid, owing to the fact that the house had 'historical interest' (IR 58/55803, no. 1344).

picture of the economic circumstances of a person. Where tithe was payable, it follows that there will be information about the property in the tithe apportionment and map.

Occasionally an entry states when the property was purchased, or when it last changed hands. The field books for Aldham in Suffolk continued to be used in the Valuation Office all through the 1920s and into the early 1930s to record dates of sale of the property (with the valuation) and sometimes the date of death of the owner. These notes are carefully dated, thus making them of much interest to those researching house and family history. Conversely, one may find a negative statement, for example 'No sale within the last twenty years'.

It is worth checking all the entries for your area, since it was still common in 1910 for branches of a family to live in the same locality, and you may find other people of the same surname living close by.

Living conditions

Many entries contain a detailed description of the property. This may include when it was built, the building materials, state of repair, number of rooms, whether there was electricity or running water. Gardens, yards, outbuildings, coal-sheds, chicken pens, fishponds and other external features are often described. Where there was a row or terrace of similar houses, there is usually a reference to the hereditament number for the first house in the row: this is where a description applicable to all the properties is to be found.

The survey's purpose was to value each unit of property. To do this, the surveyor needed to inspect the premises and take into account the difference in value between the land alone and the use currently being made of the land – whether to contain a building, to be cultivated or for some other purpose such as a recreation ground or a grouse-shooting moor. Sometimes, the surveyor used the section headed 'Particulars, description, and notes made on inspection' to give a vivid word-picture of the property. More often, the information given is formulaic, and you need to use your imagination to construct a picture of what life was like, from this raw material. From the entries, you might infer that your ancestor lived in the kind of comfort enjoyed by Rudyard Kipling at Bateman's (**IR 58/29280**): 'a detached stone & tile house . . . stone mullioned windows . . . oak panelled & beamed . . .'. Electric lighting and radiators had been installed in this house, which contained no fewer than 11 bedrooms. Or you may come to the conclusion that life was a real struggle, with people living in sub-standard and insanitary accommodation let at a rent they could barely afford. Some field books mention sanitary arrangements – 'ECs' (earth closets) in gardens or yards were then still common. Worst of all, some premises were described by the valuer as unfit for human habitation but were clearly still being used as dwellings. Whatever the picture you form, you should be able to find out what kind of house your ancestors occupied and find its precise location on a map.

Sometimes, the Ordnance Survey map depicts a road on the verge of development. Plots may be described as building-land or land set aside for housing, and there may be references to houses being built or roads under construction. The map of Whitstable, for example, shows a large area west of the railway line (Douglas Avenue, Downs Avenue and area to the south) amended in manuscript to show later roads and building plots. The corresponding field book entries (in **IR 58/17796**) indicate that in 1914 this was still undeveloped land. One of the field books relating to these small plots (**IR 58/17832**, for hereditament numbers 3901 to 4000) makes it quite clear that these plots constituted the Rayham Hill Estate, which evolved to become a most desirable residential area. Sometimes, as in this case, the records enable one to trace changes to street names: Seaview Road changed to Grasmere Road: the alteration on the map was effected by drawing an ink line through 'Seaview Road' and substituting Grasmere Road in ink alongside.

Working conditions

The Valuation Office survey applied to premises of every kind, so there are entries relating to factories, mines, quarries, warehouses, shops, forges, offices, schools, banks, and station buildings. Mills were still in common use, often rented or leased by a miller from a local landowner. There may be information about the respective ownership of the building, gearing and millstones and about the kind of equipment in the mill – for example, 'Grist mill with overshot wheel and 2 stones'. Industrial buildings may be very fully described, so that one can build up an impression of crowded, noisy working conditions or small-scale workshops. Such features as fire-escapes, cellars, strongrooms and storage areas are often noted. Minerals were separately valued, and there are separate mineral field books for mineral-rich areas such as the Forest of Dean.

Many people still worked in service, either in private houses or in hotels or inns. Descriptions of gardens, stables, dairies, laundries etc., can help to give a picture of the everyday environment of working people who helped make life pleasant for the well-to-do.

The wider community

The field books can be useful for local history, as they show the pattern of landholding across the parish. In urban areas, one can often see that large numbers of small houses were owned and rented out by a small number of landowners, and one can infer the incomes such landowners were reaping from the poorer sections of the community. In more rural villages, it is sometimes possible to form an idea of the interrelationship between local people by examining patterns of leasing parcels of land, and grazing rights, perhaps on commons. Sporting rights are described because they were considered to be a public benefit and so offset against the duty.

Entries relating to schools, churches, public houses, village halls, shops, town halls, police stations and all kinds of other buildings can help flesh out a picture of the area

London: Leman Street.

THIS fine block of buildings is the headquarters of the London Branch. The older part of the building, with the clock tower, was erected in 1887, and the new wing for the accommodation of the drapery department was opened for business in 1910. The general office, boardroom, conference-hall, dining-rooms, and kitchen are all in the older building, where also the grocery saleroom and buyers' offices are situated. The basement serves the purpose of a storeroom for provisions—cheese, butter, eggs, lard, &c.—while the upper floors are devoted to the grocery and boot and shoe departments, access being given both to the new wing and to a still older building not shown in the illustration, where the furnishing, ironmongery, carpets, and stationery departments are situated.

The latest wing is devoted to the heavy and fancy drapery, millinery, and ready-mades departments, the basement being used for a joint packing-room. At the top of the building is a telephonic exchange, which connects all the departments in London, Northampton, Bristol, Cardiff, Manchester, Newcastle, and the productive works in various parts of the country.

The building, which is 333 feet in length, is of fireproof construction, the floors being built of steel and concrete, an automatic fire-extinguishing apparatus being installed throughout. Besides three stone staircases for business purposes, iron stairways provide extra exit in case of fire. There are two electric passenger lifts, besides numerous lifts for the conveyance of goods. Electric light is provided throughout, and the building is warmed by low-pressure hot-water pipes. An efficiently-drilled fire brigade composed of members of the staff afford additional security against fire.

Figure 18 One of the Valuation Office field book entries for Whitechapel relates to the London headquarters of the Co-operative Wholesale Society: a printed drawing shows the original building erected in 1887 and the new extension opened in 1910 (IR 58/84839).

in which your forebears lived. The surveyors often made comments about the facilities in such buildings. A school in Congleton, Cheshire, with 'low and somewhat dark rooms' is summarized as 'does not meet with the approval of the education people'. Other entries relating to schools may state how many classrooms, teachers and pupils were there.

The church was still often the central focus of the community. Many churches and chapels are described in detail worthy of Pevsner: 'a stone building in Perpendicular style, comprising the nave, south porch, and embattled western tower containing three bells' is the valuer's verdict on St Petrock's church in Clannaborough, Devon. The field book also supplies the information that the church had been restored in 1858 and provided 60 sittings. Other entries relating to churches may mention lighting, heating, Sunday school rooms, even architects' names. Glebe lands, rectories, tithe barns and other ecclesiastical buildings are also identifiable. Churchyards and burial grounds may be described. There may also be a link with the tithe records when information is given in the field books about liability for tithe payments. The Down St Mary field book even tells us that the vicar had been inducted to the living in 1909.

The church represented a traditional way of life for many people. There is also evidence of newer pursuits, particularly in the towns: entries describing 'picture palaces', dance halls, swimming-baths and motor garages all testify to the spirit of this halcyon age which preceded the Great War.

Public rights of way

Although it was not one of the objects of the survey to make a systematic record of public rights of way, you may find rights of public access recorded in the field books. This is because public benefits were allowed to be offset against increment value duty, so it was in the landowner's interest to declare such rights. In such cases, the field book may contain notes about public rights of way – footpath or bridleway, for example – or access to common land. In towns, it is sometimes possible to obtain information about occupation roads in private ownership or accommodation roads giving access to industrial or commercial premises – a right of way is even recorded cutting through lawyers' chambers in central London. Sometimes a footpath is shown on the corresponding map, so the course of the right of way may be inferred. It is important to remember that the depiction of a way, path or track on a printed Ordnance Survey map does not of itself constitute evidence for the existence of a public right of way, but a map and a Valuation Office field book taken together have sometimes been accepted as such evidence by courts and tribunals.

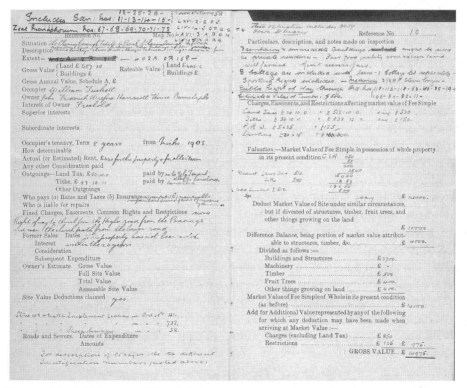

Figure 19 A Valuation Office field book entry relating to Clannaborough in Devon which provides information about rights of way (IR 58/4522).

Summary

The documents produced by the Valuation Office for the 1910 survey can take your research back to before the First World War. They can bridge the gap between the 1901 census and the National Farm Survey or the memories of living parents or grandparents. They are a rich source of detail about land ownership and land usage in early-twentieth-century England and Wales.

Other records of the Valuation Office survey

The Valuation Office survey generated an enormous amount of paperwork: some 180 forms are said to have been used! The principal surviving documents are as follows.

Valuation Books

The Valuation Books (sometimes known as 'Domesday Books') were the first major record of the hereditaments created by the Valuation Office at the commencement of the survey. They record much of the same information as the field books, but without data from the survey in the field (i.e. the descriptions and plans of land and property), and often without the assessable site value figures. Sometimes the Valuation Books include the addresses of landowners who were not occupiers.

The Valuation Books are particularly important because they can enable a hereditament number to be found when the map has not survived. All the parishes making up an income tax parish are listed in the Valuation Book, and the composition of the income tax parish is normally given on the cover of the book and is often listed as such by the local record office. This can make it straightforward to find the income tax parish in which a particular place lay. The Valuation Book also gives the range of hereditament numbers for each such parish within the income tax parish. The hereditaments are listed in numerical sequence, parish by parish, for the whole income tax parish; the Valuation Books usually provide the map reference for each hereditament. Sometimes the Valuation Books for urban areas contain detailed indexes of street and house names, and it is therefore possible to find a hereditament by its street address. The Valuation Books were used by the district valuation offices long after the repeal in 1920 of increment value duty, and they often include later amendments recording, for example, change of ownership.

The Valuation Books for the City of London and Westminster (Paddington) are held by the National Archives in record series **IR 91**. Other surviving Valuation Books are usually in local record offices. Hampshire County Record Office holds Valuation Books for certain of the areas (notably Winchester and Southampton) for which no record sheet plans or field books survive.

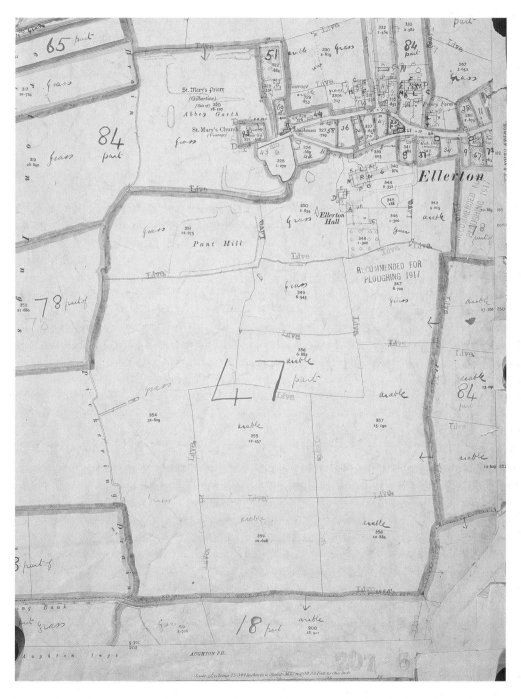

Figure 20 This example of a working plan is of Ellerton in the East Riding of Yorkshire. It shows information not required for the 1910 survey: 'live' and 'dead' boundaries, land use, and 'land recommended for ploughing 1917' (IR 134/5/368).

Working plans

Many local record offices hold Valuation Office working plans. If you cannot find the record map you require at the National Archives, it may be worth enquiring whether the appropriate local record office holds the corresponding working plan.

Form 4-Land

Sometimes entries in the field books contain no particulars, but simply the note 'See Form 4'. Details of large properties were sometimes too extensive to be entered fully in the field books, and in such cases, the Form 4-Land appears to have been retained for reference. The Forms 4-Land have not been preserved among the records of the Valuation Office – most have been destroyed – but copies retained by landowners for their own use are sometimes to be found among estate records, solicitors' papers and similar accumulations in local archives. Some local record offices have sizeable holdings. The forms are of value as they include the landowners' own descriptions of their property.

The National Archives holds sets of Forms 4-Land relating to Admiralty lands (**ADM 116/1279**), lands of the Forestry Commission (**F 6/16**) and of the Rhymney Railway Company (**RAIL 1057/1714**). The latter include copies of the instructions for completion of the forms.

Forms 36-Land and 37-Land

These forms contained the statement made by the district valuation offices of the provisional valuation of each hereditament. Form 37-Land was the statement of provisional valuation made on completion of the survey and retained in the district valuation office; a copy was sent to the landowner as Form 36-Land. A few examples of Form 36-Land relating to the Rhymney Railway Company are in **RAIL 1057/1714**. The Forms 37-Land are important because they give the exact area of each unit of land being valued, information which is not necessarily found in the field books. They also contain the addresses of landowners who were not owner-occupiers. A landowner could opt to have his land assessed by part hereditament, and the Form 37-Land is the only document that shows how such part valuation can be related to the record maps. Sometimes additional details of large estates which were not entered into the field books can be found attached to a Form 37-Land. Surviving sets of Form 37-Land are held by local record offices.

Miscellaneous records

Some other records held by the National Archives may be of interest to family and local historians seeking more background information on the implementation of the survey.

A set of papers about the land tax proposals and discussions prior to the 1909 Budget is in **IR 73/6**.

A record of each district valuation office, and the progress of the survey to the end of 1912, is in **IR 74/148**. This provides some detail on how the survey was carried out, the types of records created, the staff employed, and the premises where they worked.

An account of the Valuation Office's history and responsibilities was produced in 1920 (**IR 74/218**). It is especially useful for the background to the planning and implementation of the survey.

The calculation of increment value duty is described in **IR 83/54, T 1/11209/10949** and **T 170/4**.

Records of the Land Value Reference Committee, set up under the Act to regulate procedure in appeals against assessment, are in **LT 5**. They include registers of appeals and a few sample case files. Most of the latter appear to relate to minerals and include copies of Form 76-Land (mineral rights) and Form 77-Land (notice of appeal).

A few petitions against assessment (including special cases, awards etc.) are in **E 186**. Reports of the Inland Revenue Solicitor are in **IR 99/29–42**. Papers relating to one celebrated test case (Lady Emily Frances Smyth v Commissioners of Inland Revenue, which was concerned with the valuation of Model Farm, Norton Malreward, Somerset) are in **IR 40/2502**. Papers on the consequences of another case, Commissioners of Inland Revenue v Lumsden, are in **T 172/100**. **IR 83/54** is a file of press cuttings about individual legal cases. Other memoranda about court cases are in **T 171/39**.

Scotland

Scotland was divided into 12 Valuation Districts for the purposes of the 1910 Finance Act. The field books and maps relating to the Valuation Office survey in Scotland are held by the National Archives of Scotland: the field books in record series IRS 51–88 and the maps in IRS 101–133. More information on using these records is given in Cecil Sinclair, *Tracing Scottish Local History*, pp. 28–9.

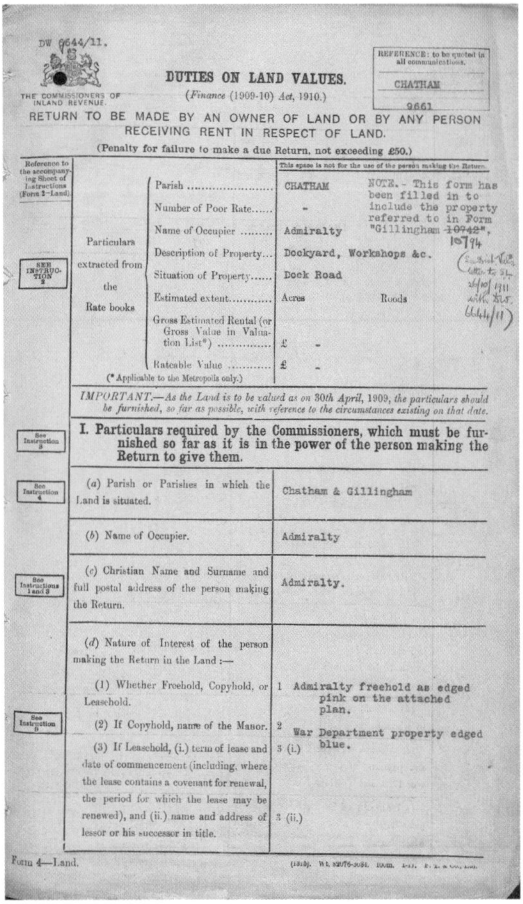

DW 6644/11.

THE COMMISSIONERS OF INLAND REVENUE.

REFERENCE: to be quoted in all communications. CHATHAM 9661

DUTIES ON LAND VALUES.

(*Finance* (1909-10) *Act*, 1910.)

RETURN TO BE MADE BY AN OWNER OF LAND OR BY ANY PERSON RECEIVING RENT IN RESPECT OF LAND.

(Penalty for failure to make a due Return, not exceeding £50.)

Reference to the accompanying Sheet of Instructions (Form 2—Land).

This space is not for the use of the person making the Return.

Particulars extracted from the Rate books	Parish	CHATHAM
	Number of Poor Rate	-
	Name of Occupier	Admiralty
	Description of Property	Dockyard, Workshops &c.
	Situation of Property	Dock Road
	Estimated extent	Acres Roods
	Gross Estimated Rental (or Gross Value in Valuation List*)	£ -
	Rateable Value	£ -

NOTE.- This form has been filled in to include the property referred to in Form "Gillingham ~~10742~~", 10794

(* Applicable to the Metropolis only.)

SEE INSTRUCTION 2

IMPORTANT.—As the Land is to be valued as on 30th April, 1909, the particulars should be furnished, so far as possible, with reference to the circumstances existing on that date.

See Instruction 3

I. Particulars required by the Commissioners, which must be furnished so far as it is in the power of the person making the Return to give them.

See Instruction 4 — (*a*) Parish or Parishes in which the Land is situated.	Chatham & Gillingham
(*b*) Name of Occupier.	Admiralty
See Instructions 1 and 5 — (*c*) Christian Name and Surname and full postal address of the person making the Return.	Admiralty.
(*d*) Nature of Interest of the person making the Return in the Land:—	
See Instruction 6 — (1) Whether Freehold, Copyhold, or Leasehold.	1 Admiralty freehold as edged pink on the attached plan.
(2) If Copyhold, name of the Manor.	2 War Department property edged blue.
(3) If Leasehold, (i.) term of lease and date of commencement (including, where the lease contains a covenant for renewal, the period for which the lease may be renewed), and (ii.) name and address of lessor or his successor in title.	3 (i.) 3 (ii.)

Form 4—Land.

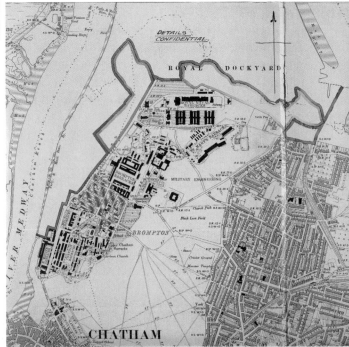

Figure 21 An example of a Valuation Office Form-4: this relates to Admiralty lands in Dock Road, Chatham, Kent (ADM 116/1279). The Admiralty retained a duplicate set of the forms they completed. The corresponding field book entry (number 9661) is in IR 58/70715.

Figure 22 A plan showing the Admiralty lands to which the Form-4 above refers.

4 The National Farm Survey of England and Wales, 1941–3

Did your ancestors work on the land during the Second World War? If so, these records may give you information about them. They are also a valuable source for local historians.

The National Farm Survey, like the Valuation Office survey before it, was dubbed a second Domesday survey, and provides a wealth of detail about farms, farmers and communities across the country, some 850 years after the first Domesday. The NFS went further than its precursor in identifying individuals working on the land, describing how they worked it and under what conditions.

Why was the survey carried out?

The National Farm Survey was carried out during the Second World War by central government. From the start of the war, Britain was faced with dire food shortages, with imports of fertilizers and foodstuffs drastically cut, so there was an urgent need for greater home food production. The area of land under cultivation had to be increased significantly and quickly. The Ministry of Agriculture and Fisheries (MAF) aimed to do this via County War Agricultural Executive Committees ('County War Ags'), who were given many powers. They could reclaim derelict land, requisition labour, tell farmers what to grow, inspect property and, in extreme cases of bad management, take possession of land. Much of the day-to-day work was carried out by district committee members, who were usually local farmers themselves. In the film *The Land Girls*, a man from one of these committees is shown telling the reluctant farmer to plough up his pasture land and convert it to arable, which gives an opportunity to show one of the glamorous girls learning to drive a tractor. A farm survey was made to assist the ploughing-up campaign, which extended to land that had not seen the plough since medieval or even prehistoric times. Between June 1940 and the early months of 1941 all but the smallest farms were surveyed, and classified according to the physical condition of the land and productivity as A, B or C. Only summary statistics survive from this survey.

Once the short-term objective of increasing food production had been achieved, a second survey was made with a longer-term goal, to inform postwar agricultural planning. This was the National Farm Survey, taken between spring 1941 and the end of 1943. It was envisaged as a permanent and comprehensive record of the conditions on the farms of England and Wales, although the thrust of the questions asked was still towards ensuring that the land was used for maximum output, and that it was managed efficiently. The National Farm Survey was destined to become part of the national archive at the Public Record Office, where the 'second Domesday survey' would join the first.

What places did it cover?

The National Farm Survey had a wide remit. It covered all agricultural areas of five acres and above in England and Wales: some 300,000 holdings. These ranged from large farms to market- and hop-gardens, and applied to many smallholders such as bulb growers and domestic poultry-keepers, who might not have called themselves farmers. If your ancestors worked on the land during the war, particularly before the end of 1943, there is a chance that they may have been recorded in the survey, to some degree. The records are useful for those studying a particular community, especially in rural areas, including some long since swallowed up by urban development.

Records of the National Farm Survey

The records produced for the National Farm Survey provide a wealth of detailed information about mid-twentieth-century rural England and Wales, including tenure and size of farms, acreage farmed, herd and flock size, farm labour, standard and methods of farming, facilities (electricity/water), equipment, horses and (their replacement) tractors, and even weeds and pests.

The Survey consisted of three elements for each farm:

- a **map** showing the farm boundaries and the fields contained in it
- a number of **farm census return forms** as at 4 June 1941, sent to farmers and filled in by them, for return to the committees
- a **primary farm record**, compiled by an inspector, who visited each farm.

Each part of the Survey for a given farm bears that farm's unique code, made up of an abbreviation of the county name, the parish number, and the individual farm number, and so links all these disparate parts of the survey. For example, **NK 531/7** comprises the abbreviation for the county of Norfolk, followed by the parish number 531 for Stiffkey, and then the individual farm number of 7 for Old Hall Farm. Occasionally you will find a fourth part added to the reference, e.g. **ST 173/255/2**; the extra number, in this case 173, is added after the letters, and is the code number of the Crop Reporter, added to the reference for Abbey Farm (farm number 2) in Muchelney (parish 255), Somerset. (See pp. 76–7.)

The maps need to be ordered separately from the textual records, under a different document reference: you can order them both at the same time, to use them together. You may wish to consult the map first:

- for a large parish, where you want to obtain the individual farm code accorded by the Survey, to save looking through large numbers of forms
- if you do not know the name or parish of your farm but just the approximate area where it lay (especially if it is an area since urbanized).

The maps (MAF 73)

The maps produced as part of the Survey, in the record series **MAF 73**, show where the farm lay and its extent, serving as a graphic index to the textual records. Although based on published Ordnance Survey maps, the unique value of these maps lies in the manuscript additions: colouring to show which fields and areas belonged to each farm, and notes giving the map sheet numbers of farm parcels shown on other map sheets. The farms are often not named on the map, but each bears a unique code, which enables you to link the plots with the textual part of the survey.

The maps were based on Ordnance Survey 25-inch sheets reduced to half size at about 12.5 inches to the mile or 1:5280, or on six-inch sheets (1:10,560). Such maps were in short supply and had to be copied. Then, the farm details were copied on to the maps. The work was done to differing standards; the extent of the farm may be shown by a colour wash over the whole farm, or it may have just its boundaries coloured. The unique farm code was added to each farm, in black ink. There may be a complication with the six-inch sheets, since the Survey required that each Ordnance Survey parcel number be taken from a 25-inch sheet and added to the six-inch sheets in manuscript, creating potential confusion between OS parcel numbers and farm codes, also added in manuscript. To guard against this, the draughtsmen would sometimes use the margins of a six-inch sheet to provide a colour-coded key to the farm holdings and their codes, and write the OS parcel numbers on the map itself. However, not all six-inch map sheets were completed to these high standards.

These maps were meant to be record sheets rather than working maps, and to be kept at the committee offices. However, it seems that some maps were taken out into the field, for they bear pencilled notes about successive farmers, changes in farm names, areas of allotments, commons or sports grounds, building and industrial development or military requisition, such as airfield construction. Such manuscript annotations can give some indication of non-agricultural land between farms, describing changes in land use since the map was printed.

How to find and use the maps in MAF 73

1. To find the reference for a map, consult the volume of index map sheets for **MAF 73**, which bears the document reference **MAF 73/64**, and is kept in the map reference cabinet in the Map and Large Document Reading Room. The index sheets are arranged in county alphabetical order for England, then Wales. These sheets show topographical detail to help you identify the right area, including parish names

and boundaries; you may find a magnifying glass helpful when looking at these sheets, since the background detail can be faint. The index sheets have a superimposed grid, which enables you to find the reference to Ordnance Survey sheets at the scales of 1:2500 and six inches to a mile.

2. When you find the right place, note the large stamped number added to the index sheet in the lower right-hand corner (being careful not to take the reference from the sheet underneath, if you are looking at a small sheet). This number forms the second component of the document reference you will need to order your map, the first being that of the series, **MAF 73**, so that, if you are looking for the map for Kew, you will now have **MAF 73/40**, the 40 standing for the county of Surrey.

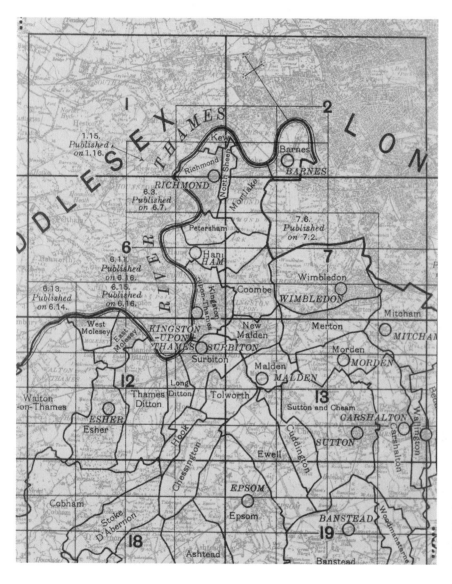

Figure 23 Part of the National Farm Survey key sheet for Surrey, showing Kew (MAF 73/64).

3. Next, note the number in the centre of the large grid rectangle in which your area falls. The format for the map reference is the series **MAF 73** plus the county number (or part of larger counties – see the section below on the **MAF 73** series list if you are searching for places in Lincolnshire, Suffolk, Sussex or Yorkshire) plus the grid number: thus, **MAF 73**/county number/grid number. For example, if wanting the map for Kew, the number in the centre of the large rectangle in which Kew falls is 1, so **MAF 73/40/1** is the full reference needed to order the set of maps relating to the numbered rectangle for Surrey in which Kew lies.

4. The National Farm Survey maps are produced as a set of maps in a folder, in the Map and Large Document Reading Room. Before ordering, you may want to determine which sheet you will need to look at, once your folder has arrived. If the maps are 25-inch (reduced), then there will be 16 sheets corresponding to the area within the numbered grid. The small rectangles representing these sheets are not individually numbered on the index sheet, but once you have found the square in which your farm falls, you can mentally number the squares along the rows from the top left-hand corner to the bottom right. For a six-inch map, there are four quarter-sheets, arranged from NW to SE (see the diagrams in Chapter 5).

When you receive the folder of maps that you have ordered, you will see that the maps are arranged in numerical order, 1–16 (if 25-inch), or from NW to SE (if six-inch). Please be careful to replace the maps in this order. The inside flap of the folder is stamped with an index grid for the particular rectangle showing which maps are included. Go to the sheet you require, the number of which you obtained by mentally numbering the large grid on the index sheet. The farm you are seeking will be identified on the map by its unique code. Note the (civil) parish in which the farm lay, if you do not already have this information, as you will need it for ordering the forms. If your farm had any other lands which are shown on adjacent map sheets, this will normally be indicated by the appropriate Ordnance Survey map reference.

The MAF 73 series list

The series list for **MAF 73** (in paper form or online) does not provide map reference numbers, but can be used to see the counties set out with their piece numbers and the number ranges of the Ordnance Survey sheets for each county. The list shows where the sheets for complete numbered rectangles are 'wanting', for the mapping is not complete. Some maps were never made, some were lost before transfer to the Public Record Office (possibly through the kind of field trips mentioned above), and no maps were made for urban areas with no agricultural land. Places most liable to 'wanting' maps are in County Durham, Monmouthshire, and the Scilly Isles. The list also shows some numbers marked 'not used', for central urban areas with no agricultural land.

The series list also gives the separate numbers assigned to administrative subdivisions of large counties. The counties in question are:

- Lincolnshire – parts of Holland (23), Kesteven (24), and Lindsey (25)
- Suffolk – east (38), west (39)
- Sussex – east (41), west (42)
- Yorkshire – Ridings: east (47), north (48), west (49).

London is a special case: although there is an index sheet for London, there are no maps orderable under the respective reference 26 – you will be referred to the maps for Middlesex, some of which cover the same area. Note, too, that there are separate sections for the Isle of Ely, the Isle of Wight and the Soke of Peterborough.

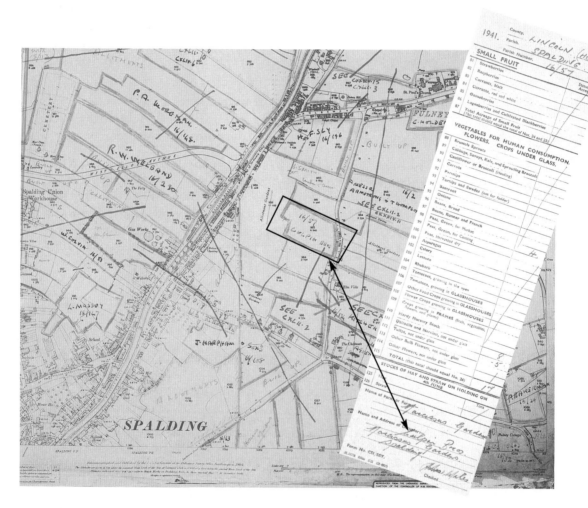

Figure 24   The National Farm Survey included market gardens and bulb fields, as seen here at Spalding in Lincolnshire (MAF 73/23/134 sheet 14 and MAF 32/788/16 farm number 57 for the Culpin Brothers' Narcissus Gardens).

The textual records: MAF 32

The textual records for each parish are held together in the record series **MAF 32**, arranged by county and parish. They take the form of four printed forms, usually arranged in the following order:

a. A return of small fruit, vegetables, bulbs and flowers, and stocks of hay and straw.
b. A return of agricultural land, providing details of crops and grass acreage, livestock numbers (including horses), and labour employed on the farm.
c. The primary farm record obtained mainly in the field by inspection and by interviewing the farmer. The two dates on the double-sided form show when the field information was recorded, and when the form was completed in the office.
d. A further return, with additional questions on labour, motive power such as horses and tractors, rent payable, and how many years the farmer had occupied the farm.

The farm census returns

The three 'census' forms (a, b and d) were posted to the farmer, for completion on 4 June 1941, and return to the committee. There are sometimes only two census forms for a particular farm. Whereas the first two forms were familiar to farmers as they were required to be completed each year, the third, 'supplementary' form was issued only in 1941, and some farmers apparently were not willing to fill in yet another form, or to answer questions which asked for details on more delicate matters such as the workforce, including the farmer's family, the value of the farm and the rent paid. Although 60,000 first reminders were issued, demanding the completion of the extra forms, many are absent.

The primary farm record

This was written by an inspector in the field, who interviewed the farmer, and recorded what he saw around him. The inspector was armed with a printed form on which to note this information, with boxes for him to tick. There was space on the back of the form for any comments the inspector might wish to make; in many cases these are left blank, but there may be comments on farming methods, on the tenure of the farm, or on the farmer. Information is given on crops, tenure and the natural condition of the farm (fertility, drainage, derelict areas, weed and pest prevalence); adequacy of buildings, equipment, water and electricity supplies. Farmers were classified according to how well they were perceived to be managing the farm and its resources. Nationally, 58% of farmers received an A rating, indicating that they were good managers; 37% received a B rating, suggesting that they were farming fairly well; and 5% were marked 'C', which indicates that some 15,000 farms were poorly managed. A good farmer could merit an A grade despite managing a farm of low productivity because of poor soils. This classification system was unevenly applied throughout the country, it seems; some

Figure 25a The National Farm Survey map for Abbey Farm at Muchelney, Somerset. Note the farm number (255/2) at the centre of the map (MAF 73/36/72).

FARM SURVEY

County Code No. 255

County *Somerset*

Code No. *ST/173/255/2*

District *5*

Parish *Muchelney*

Name of holding *ABBEY FARM*

Name of farmer *CRIDLAND, P.J.*

Address of farmer *Abbey Farm Muchelney Taunton*

Number and edition of 6-inch Ordnance Survey Sheet containing farmstead *LXXII SE Ed 1931*

A. TENURE.

1. Is occupier tenant — ☓
   owner

2. If tenant, name and address of owner :—
   E.R.S. Cridland
   The Parsonage
   Muchelney

3. Is farmer full time farmer — ☓
   part time farmer
   spare time farmer
   hobby farmer
   other type
   Other occupation, if any :—

	Yes	No
4. Does farmer occupy other land ?		☓

Name of Holding	County	Parish

	Yes	No
5. Has farmer grazing rights over land not occupied by him ?		☓
If so, nature of such rights—		

B. CONDITIONS OF FARM.

	Heavy	Medium	Light	Peaty
1. Proportion (%) of area on which soil is		100		

2. Is farm conveniently laid out ? Yes ... ☓
   Moderately
   No ...

	Good	Fair	Bad
3. Proportion (%) of farm which is naturally	80	20	
4. Situation in regard to road	☓		
5. Situation in regard to railway	☓		
6. Condition of farmhouse	☓		
Condition of buildings	☓		
7. Condition of farm roads		☓	
8. Condition of fences	☓		
9. Condition of ditches	☓		
10. General condition of field drainage	☓		
11. Condition of cottages	☓		

	No.
12. Number of cottages within farm area	2
Number of cottages elsewhere	
13. Number of cottages let on service tenancy	1

	Yes	No
14. Is there infestation with :—		
rabbits and moles		☓
rats and mice		☓
rooks and wood pigeons	☓	
other birds		☓
insect pests		☓
15. Is there heavy infestation with weeds ?		☓
If so, kinds of weeds :—		

	Yes	No
16. Are there derelict fields ?		☓
If so, acreage		

C. WATER AND ELECTRICITY.

	Pipe	Well	Roof	Stream	None
Water supply :—					
1. To farmhouse	☓				
2. To farm buildings	☓				
3. To fields				☓	

	Yes	No
4. Is there a seasonal shortage of water ?		☓
Electricity supply :—		
5. Public light		☓
Public power		☓
Private light		☓
Private power		☓
6. Is it used for household purposes ?		☓
Is it used for farm purposes ?		☓

D. MANAGEMENT.

1. Is farm classified as A, B or C ? — *A*

2. Reasons for B or C :—
   old age
   lack of capital
   personal failings

   If personal failings, details :—

	Good	Fair	Poor	Bad
3. Condition of arable land	☓			
4. Condition of pasture	☓			

	Adequate	To some extent	Not at all
5. Use of fertilisers on :—			
arable land	☓		
grass land	☓		

Field information recorded by

D.J. Stewart

Date of recording *27.10.42*

This primary record completed by

E. Cockell

Date *10.12.42*

Form No. B496/E.I.

*15946. Wt.46166/817. 3000 pads. 3/41. Wy.L.P. Gp.676.

Figure 25b The National Farm Survey inspector's report on Abbey Farm at Muchelney, Somerset. Note the farm number (255/2) at the top right of the form (MAF 32/144/255).

complete parishes within certain counties have straight runs of A farms, and others of B. Some inspectors apparently had difficulty distinguishing between a farm which was poorly managed, and one which was simply on bad land, perhaps because the survey of 1940–41 had graded the farm rather than the farmer. This new assessment of the farmer was a controversial part of the Survey, and the one for which it is often remembered.

How to find and use the records in MAF 32

The full reference to order the individual farm records for a parish comprises the series reference **MAF 32**, plus the piece number plus the parish number; e.g. **MAF 32/1315/39** is the reference for the farm records for the parish of Betws-y-coed in Caernarvonshire. Please note, however, that the format for places in Warwickshire is more complicated, containing part numbers in the piece reference; for instance, the reference for records of Baddesley Clinton is **MAF 32/956 Pt.1/201**.

You can get the reference for the textual records in advance of your visit, by using the search facility on the online catalogue from our website, specifying your parish in the search field and the series **MAF 32** in the reference field. This is also the easiest way to get a reference during your visit, via the computer terminals in the reading rooms.

If you prefer, you can also get the reference by using the paper series list for MAF 32 at the National Archives. The records are listed by county (but for split counties, London, the Isle of Ely, the Isle of Wight and the Soke of Peterborough, see the section earlier entitled 'The **MAF 73** series list', since all of these areas are listed separately). The counties are not arranged alphabetically, so you will first need to consult the index to the counties which precedes the series list, and gives the piece ranges for each county. The records are arranged alphabetically by parish within each county. Make a note of the number to the left of your parish name, which is the parish code number, and of the number in the far left-hand column under which your parish is grouped with several other parishes; this is the piece number. The full reference is **MAF 32**/piece number/parish number.

If you have difficulty in finding your parish name listed, you can search the **MAF 32** series list under the particular county until you find the parish which bears the parish code number you have obtained from the map.

The farm records for each parish are kept loose within large envelopes or folders, which are labelled with the parish name and the parish code number. The records for each farm are not grouped together, but rather the forms are grouped into the separate types; all the primary farm records together and all the census returns filed by type. Within these groups the forms are arranged in numerical sequence by the farm codes. You will need to look in each part for the record for your farm. There may be up to a hundred farms in a parish, each with multiple forms. If you have the code for your farm, which you have taken from the relevant map, you can go directly to the forms for your farm. Each part of the farm record also gives the name of the farm and of the farmer and his address, so that, if it is a small parish, it will be easy to find the relevant forms. If you do not have the farm code and it is a large parish, find the map for the area in question (see p. 71), from which you can identify the farm code. Please do not change the order in which you find the documents. If they appear to be in the wrong order, please notify a member of staff in the Reading Room.

What kind of information can the National Farm Survey provide for family and local historians?

There is a wealth of detail in the records, although variable from county to county, and between different inspectors. The usefulness of the information for family history varies from case to case, but there can be quite a lot about the farmer.

Farm owners

The names and addresses of farm owners are given, where different from the occupier, on the primary farm record. Occasionally, one name is crossed out and another entered, reflecting the fact that the farm had changed ownership. There is rarely any extra information about the owner, but a glance through the other forms for that parish will show if other holdings were owned by the same person. A farmer might own several farms, but just keep one to work himself. Large landowners might own a number of farms in the parish. This was the case with Vita Sackville-West, cited as the 'Hon Mrs V. M. Nicolson' in the owner's slot on the primary record for a number of farms in Kent, while the supplementary form for Sissinghurst Castle, for which she was the 'farmer', was returned without an estimate of rental value, deemed 'impossible to estimate, as much of it is a pleasure garden'. You may find owners described as 'the executors of the deceased's estate', particularly useful as the forms are dated.

Farmers

The forms give the farmer's address and name, often with a number of initials, which may help to distinguish between two people with a common surname. For lady farmers, nobility and military personnel, the full title is given. These were the people named as farming the holding, whether as owner or occupier. The farmers' handwriting on some of the forms may give some idea of their character and education. The inspectors' forms can fill out this picture. Comment was rarely made on farmers who were classed A. The most likely reasons for a lower mark were old age or infirmity, lack of capital, or 'personal failings'. Old age rarely elicited particular comment, although two sisters were marked down from A to B through age, with the note 'two old ladies'. In addition to actual infirmity, such as poor health or loss of a limb, physical incapacity might also cover the decease of a farmer, leaving his widow to carry on. Lack of capital might also cover lack of labour or equipment, which the farmer could not help; but a lower marking might reflect on the farmer's parsimony: 'does not like parting with money'. The comment 'lack of proper implements' (in one case made of a Mr Mallett!) shows that in some places farming remained in a pre-mechanized age.

Since 'personal failings' encompassed a wide range of possibilities, from the lazy, ignorant or ineffective to the plain incapable or even the habitual drunk, inspectors were required to say more in these cases (although they did not always do so). Some used favourite stock phrases: 'lack of best farming methods' and 'lack of initiative'.

Others were more forthcoming, and there may be such comments about the farmer's character as 'lack of ability', 'lack of energy', 'easy-going' and even 'rather dilatory – spends too much time running about'. The inclusion of such remarks made this section of the survey very contentious, and to ensure confidentiality, the records were closed to public inspection for 50 instead of the usual 30 years, and only became available to the public in 1992. Researchers are likely to find more written about farmers with 'failings' than about those without. Women farmers were especially likely to receive inspectors' comments, although many were given good ratings. One lady was marked down for 'no obvious reasons', another because she 'lacks the strength of a man'.

The A classification was usually deemed sufficient comment upon a farmer's abilities, but inspectors might also make favourable remarks, regardless of ratings given. 'Farms well', 'capable', and 'hard worker' are fairly common. Improvements were noted, whether made by a new arrival, or since the previous year's inspection. Even a C marking may be accompanied by a fairly positive comment: 'has the means mentally and financially to farm properly'.

The inspectors' forms note whether the farmer was full-time: if not, any other occupation is listed. Part-time farmers were more likely to attract the inspector's disapproval and lower markings, in view of the nation's need for more food, and this can mean that more information is given about them. In these cases, a C marking might not mean an incompetent or lazy farmer, simply one with another job, with not enough time to do both properly. This may be another reason that Mr Mallett got a C marking, as he was also a butcher.

Many of the occupations given are of a rural nature: wheelwright, vermin destroyer, seed merchant, miller, carpenter, thatcher. There are also more apparently urban occupations: undertaker, company director, engineer, train driver, stockbroker, government official. This is particularly the case in areas near towns and cities, where many people kept smallholdings and market gardens, in addition to other jobs. One fairly common main occupation, in town and country, was that of innkeeper; this usually took precedence over tilling any land kept around the inn.

The comments 'retired', 'widower' or 'widow' may be placed under the occupation head. For married women farmers, the occupation of their husband may be given here: for example, a London businessman. Other background information is occasionally found, here or elsewhere on the form; perhaps that the farmer was a retired army officer, had been ill, had a son in the police force, or lost an arm in the First World War, which may lead you to other records.

A useful piece of information, given on the supplementary census form, is the length of time the farmer had held the farm. He or she might have arrived too recently to be assessed, or have farmed that land for decades. In some cases the land is said to have been in one family since the turn of the century.

Farmers' relatives

These may not be mentioned at all, or you may be lucky, and find some reference to them, although names and ages are unlikely to be given. There was a section on the supplementary census form to record specified relatives of the farmer and his wife, who worked on the farm: father, mother, son, daughter, brother or sister. However, space was only provided to show numbers of male and female family workers, with no distinction between the farmer's relatives and those of his wife. It was not clear whether this space was meant to include the farmer and his wife: some farmers clarified matters by writing for example 'self, wife and son'; or by crossing out the non-relevant relatives printed on the form. There was also confusion between this section and the one for employed labour, on the crops return form. This may occasionally reveal useful information, especially about men; sometimes the farmer recorded his son in the employed labour section, with a tick in the relevant age-range box, which was not required on the form for family workers.

Mention of relatives may occasionally be found in the comments section on the inspector's form. In one case, the farmer was an officer away in the RAF (which was listed as 'other occupation'), and his brother was now running the farm. In another case, the farmer was described as old and feeble, but his son was doing the work.

It is worth checking all the inspectors' forms for your farmer's parish, since farming was often a family affair, and you may find other people of the same surname listed as neighbouring farmers, or as farm owners. A lady might own land farmed by her husband; sons farm for parents; and brothers occupy adjacent farms. Clues may also be found where a son or sons are named in partnership with their father or mother, for example 'Messrs J. Harpham and Sons'.

Farm workers

Farm workers are unlikely to be mentioned by name, but if you have the name of the farm, you can get some idea of what it was like to work there, how many other workers were employed, and what kind of work they did, according to the type of farm. If the farm is recorded as having farm cottages, you can picture your ancestors living in one of them. Employed workers (non-family of the farmer) were recorded at the bottom of the left-hand column on the crop and livestock return: just their sex and for the men, their age group: under 18, 18–21 or over 21, if they worked full-time. Unsurprisingly, where age is specified, the men farm workers were mostly either rather young or getting old.

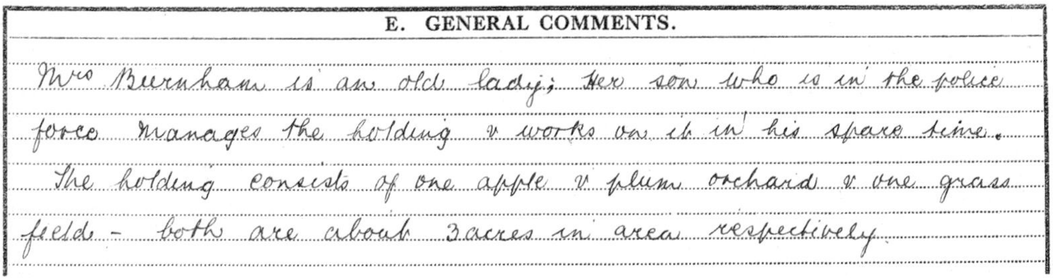
E. GENERAL COMMENTS.

Mrs Burnham is an old lady; her son who is in the police force manages the holding & works on it in his spare time. The holding consists of one apple & plum orchard & one grass field - both are about 3 acres in area respectively.

Figure 26 An example where the comments section on the back of an inspector's report gives information about a farmer's relative: an orchard in Cranbrook, Kent, was farmed by the elderly owner's policeman son (MAF 32/32/1022, farm number 101/24).

47¼acres.

FARM SURVEY

County Devon — Code No. 445/44
District 8 — Parish Pinhoe
Name of holding Remand Home. — Name of farmer Bradley. W. (Headmaster) (for Home Office)
Address of farmer " " Whipton, Exeter.
Number and edition of 6-inch Ordnance Survey Sheet containing farmstead 80 NE 1932 REV

A. TENURE.

1. Is occupier tenant	
owner (Home Office) ...	X
2. If tenant, name and address of owner :—	
3. Is farmer full time farmer	X
part time farmer	
spare time farmer	
hobby farmer	
other type	≠

Other occupation, if any :— Market Gardens etc

	Yes	No
4. Does farmer occupy other land ?		X

Name of Holding	County	Parish

C. WATER AND ELECTRICITY.

Water supply :—	Pipe	Well	Roof	Stream	None
1. To farmhouse ...	X				
2. To farm buildings ...	X				
3. To fields	X				

	Yes	No
4. Is there a seasonal shortage of water ?...		X
Electricity supply :—		
5. Public light	X	
Public power		X
Private light		X
Private power		X
6. Is it used for household purposes ? ...	X	
Is it used for farm purposes ?		X

D. MANAGEMENT.

Figure 27a The National Farm Survey included many places not normally considered to be farms. The reformatory school at Pinhoe near Exeter had enough market garden to merit assessment, and the headmaster was listed as the 'farmer' on the inspector's report (MAF 32/687/445, farm number 445/44).

Fill in both Forms 398/S.S. (Green) and C 47/S.S.Y. (Blue)

MINISTRY OF AGRICULTURE AND FISHERIES.

THE DEFENCE REGULATIONS, 1939, AND THE AGRICULTURAL RETURNS ORDER, 1939.

RETURN WITH RESPECT TO AGRICULTURAL LAND ON 4th JUNE, 1941.

	CROPS AND GRASS	Statute Acres
1	Wheat	–
2	Barley	–
3	Oats	–
4	Mixed Corn with Wheat in mixture	–
5	Mixed Corn without Wheat in mixture	–
6	Rye	–
7	Beans, winter or spring, for stock feeding	–
8	Peas, for stock feeding, not for human consumption	–
9	Potatoes, first earlies	1¼
10	Potatoes, main crop and second earlies	4¾
11	Turnips and Swedes, for fodder	1
12	Mangolds	2.
13	Sugar Beet	–
14	Kale, for fodder	–
15	Rape (or Cole)	–
16	Cabbage, Savoys, and Kohl Rabi, for fodder	–
17	Vetches or Tares	–
18	Lucerne	–
19	Mustard, for seed	–
20	Mustard, for fodder or ploughing in	–
21	Flax, for fibre or linseed	–
22	Hops, Statute Acres, not Hop Acres	–
23	Orchards, with crops, fallow, or grass below the trees	–
24	Orchards, with small fruit below the trees	–
25	Small Fruit, not under orchard trees	¼
26	Vegetables for human consumption (excluding Potatoes), Flowers and Crops under Glass	17½
27	All Other Crops not specified elsewhere on this return or grown on patches of less than ¼ acre	–
28	Bare Fallow	–
29	Clover, Sainfoin, and Temporary Grasses for Mowing this season	–
30	Clover, Sainfoin, and Temporary Grasses for Grazing (not for Mowing this season)	–
31	Permanent Grass for Mowing this season	10
32	Permanent Grass for Grazing (not for Mowing this season), but excluding rough grazings	10½
33	TOTAL OF ABOVE ITEMS, 1 to 32 (Total acreage of Crops and Grass, excluding Rough Grazings)	47¼
34	Rough Grazings—Mountain, Heath, Moor, or Down Land, or other rough land used for grazing on which the occupier has the sole grazing rights	

LABOUR actually employed on holding on **4th June.** The occupier, his wife, or domestic servants should not be entered.

			Number (in figures)
35	WHOLETIME REGULAR WORKERS	Males, 21 years old and over	2
36		Males, 18 to 21 years old	–
37	If none, write "None"	Males, under 18 years old	–
38		Women and Girls	–
39	CASUAL (SEASONAL or PART-TIME) WORKERS	Males, 21 years old and over	–
40		Males, under 21 years old	24
41		Women and Girls	–
42		TOTAL WORKERS	26

Form No. C 47/S.S.Y.

M.14060. 4/41. (52-4551)

	LIVE STOCK on holding on 4th June, including any sent for sale on that or previous day		Number (in figures)
43	Cows and Heifers in milk		4
44	Cows in Calf, but not in milk		–
45	Heifers in Calf, with first Calf		1
46	Bulls being used for service		–
47	Bulls (including Bull Calves) being reared for service		–
48	OTHER CATTLE	2 years old and above — Male	–
49		2 years old and above — Female	–
50		1 year old and under 2 — Male	–
51		1 year old and under 2 — Female	3
52		Under 1 year old:— (a) For rearing (excluding Bull Calves being reared for service)	3
53		(b) Intended for slaughter as Calves	–
54		TOTAL CATTLE and CALVES	11
55	Steers and Heifers over 1 year old being fattened for slaughter before 30th November, 1941		
56	SHEEP OVER 1 YEAR OLD	Ewes kept for further breeding (excluding two-tooth Ewes)	–
57		Rams kept for service	–
58		Two-tooth Ewes (Shearling Ewes or Gimmers) to be put to the ram in 1941	–
59		Other Sheep over 1 year old	–
60	SHEEP UNDER 1 YEAR OLD	Ewe Lambs to be put to the ram in 1941	–
61		Ram Lambs for service in 1941	–
62		Other Sheep and Lambs under 1 year old	2
63		TOTAL SHEEP and LAMBS	2
64	Sows in Pig		–
65	Gilts in Pig		–
66	Other Sows kept for breeding		3
67	Barren Sows for fattening		1
68	Boars being used for service		–
69	ALL OTHER PIGS (not entered above)	Over 5 months old	–
70		2—5 months	1
71		Under 2 months	–
72		TOTAL PIGS	5
73	POULTRY	Fowls over 6 months old	20
74		Fowls under 6 months old	10
75	If none, write "None"	Ducks of all ages	–
76		Geese of all ages	–
77		Turkeys over 6 months old	–
78		Turkeys under 6 months old	–
79		TOTAL POULTRY	30
80	GOATS OF ALL AGES		–

	HORSES on holding on 4th June		Number (in figures)
81	Horses used for Agricultural Purposes (including Mares kept for breeding) or by Market Gardeners	(a) mares	–
82		(b) geldings	2
83	Unbroken Horses of 1 year old and above	(a) mares	–
84		(b) geldings	–
85	Light Horses under 1 year old		–
86	Heavy Horses under 1 year old		–
87	Stallions being used for service in 1941		–
88	All Other Horses (not entered above)		–
89		TOTAL HORSES	2

Figure 27b The workers in the market gardens at Pinhoe were the boys in the remand home: the numbers of boys are given on the lower section of the crop form, on which male workers were enumerated by age range.

Life on the farm

The Survey's purpose was to investigate farm conditions and how farms were being managed. Occasionally, the inspector used the General Comments section of his report to give a vivid word-picture of the farm and its state of cultivation. More often, the information given is formulaic, and you need to use your imagination to construct a picture of what life was like, from this raw material. From the forms, made so that the inspector could quickly tick 'yes' or 'no', 'good' or 'bad', you might surmise that your farmer had a farm on good soil, with sound buildings and well-made roads, electricity, running water and a tractor. Or you may come to the conclusion that life was a real struggle, with buildings falling down, poor soil in scattered fields plagued by weeds and pests, with no power beyond the farmer's own strength, and just a pond or well from which to get water. Whatever the picture you form, you will be able to find out what crops were grown and which animals were kept, even the type of tractor, if there was one. Sometimes the inspector gave overall descriptions of the farm, such as 'a useful little holding' or 'a generally untidy farm'.

The survey tells us much about methods of farming, the work done, and how it was done. The inspector may say that an accredited herd was kept, or that hedging, ditching and draining were being carried out. He noted any grass fields which had been ploughed up and turned into arable land for the 1940 and 1941 harvests. The inspector's main criterion was the yield; whether the farm was producing as much food as it could. If not, he might make recommendations, or ask an expert from the committee to visit and give advice. There is often much more written in these cases, than on the many farmers whose work was commended. Sometimes the comments reflect the inspector's pet interests: he may keep saying that more labour had to be employed, or that the land 'lacks manure'.

Occasionally there is information incidental to the survey, but helpful to the historian. A conscientious inspector might record 'bungalow' against the question on the condition of the farm house, and since his report was dated, this gives a fixed point by which it must have been built. Local events may be referred to, such as a flood, or in one case, it was explained that the farm buildings were rated 'bad' due to enemy action, so one could look for newspaper reports on this. It was also noted where farm land was given up for military purposes.

The wider community

These forms can be useful for local history, as they show the acreage under particular crops across the parish, including flax, hops and other specialist crops. One can see at this particular date the size and tenure of farms, herd and flock sizes, and the prevalence of mixed farming. There are details on the make of tractor and the horsepower of other engines, including fixed ones. It is clear that many farms were still without electricity and piped water. One can see the incidence of farm labour; if there is a pattern in the condition of buildings, drainage and hedges, say across a single estate; even which weeds and pests were prevalent in the area. The inspector's report comments on the farm's situation with regard to road and railway and the

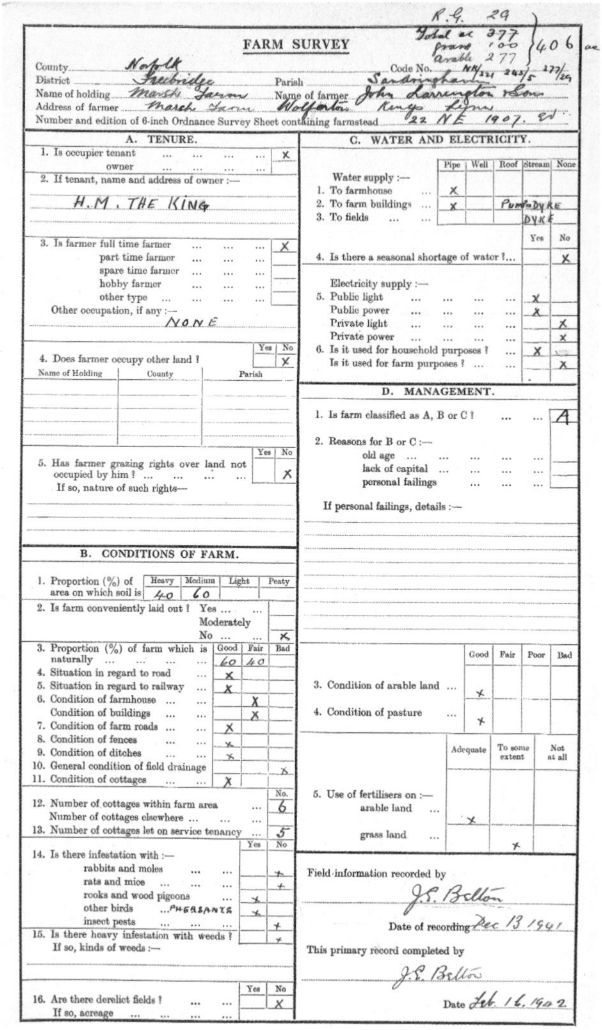

R.G. 29

FARM SURVEY

Total ac 377 / grass 100 / arable 277 } 406 ac

County: Norfolk — Code No. NK/321 245/5 277/29
District: Freebridge — Parish: Sandringham
Name of holding: Marsh Farm — Name of farmer: John Larrington & Son
Address of farmer: Marsh Farm Wolferton Kings Lynn
Number and edition of 6-inch Ordnance Survey Sheet containing farmstead: 22 NE 1907. Ed.

A. TENURE.

1. Is occupier tenant ... X
   owner ...
2. If tenant, name and address of owner :— H.M. THE KING
3. Is farmer full time farmer ... X
   part time farmer ...
   spare time farmer ...
   hobby farmer ...
   other type ...
   Other occupation, if any :— NONE
4. Does farmer occupy other land? Yes / No: X

Name of Holding	County	Parish

5. Has farmer grazing rights over land not occupied by him? ... Yes / No: X
   If so, nature of such rights—

B. CONDITIONS OF FARM.

1. Proportion (%) of area on which soil is

Heavy	Medium	Light	Peaty
40	60		

2. Is farm conveniently laid out? Yes ... / Moderately / No ... X

	Good	Fair	Bad
3. Proportion (%) of farm which is naturally ...	60	40	
4. Situation in regard to road ...	X		
5. Situation in regard to railway ...	X		
6. Condition of farmhouse ...		X	
Condition of buildings ...		X	
7. Condition of farm roads ...	X		
8. Condition of fences ...	X		
9. Condition of ditches ...	X		
10. General condition of field drainage			X
11. Condition of cottages ...	X		

	No.
12. Number of cottages within farm area ...	6
Number of cottages elsewhere ...	
13. Number of cottages let on service tenancy ...	5

14. Is there infestation with :—	Yes	No
rabbits and moles ...		X
rats and mice ...		X
rooks and wood pigeons ...	X	
other birds ...PHEASANTS	X	
insect pests ...		X
15. Is there heavy infestation with weeds?		X

If so, kinds of weeds :—

	Yes	No
16. Are there derelict fields? ...		X
If so, acreage ...		

C. WATER AND ELECTRICITY.

Water supply :—	Pipe	Well	Roof	Stream	None
1. To farmhouse ...	X				
2. To farm buildings ...	X		PUMP	DYKE	
3. To fields ...				DYKE	

	Yes	No
4. Is there a seasonal shortage of water? ...		X
Electricity supply :—		
5. Public light ...	X	
Public power ...	X	
Private light ...		X
Private power ...		X
6. Is it used for household purposes? ...	X	
Is it used for farm purposes? ...		X

D. MANAGEMENT.

1. Is farm classified as A, B or C? ... A
2. Reasons for B or C :—
   old age ...
   lack of capital ...
   personal failings ...

If personal failings, details :—

	Good	Fair	Poor	Bad
3. Condition of arable land ...	X			
4. Condition of pasture ...	X			

5. Use of fertilisers on :—	Adequate	To some extent	Not at all
arable land ...	X		
grass land ...		X	

Field information recorded by J.S. Belton

Date of recording Dec 13 1941

This primary record completed by J.S. Belton

Date Feb. 16, 1942.

Figure 28 There was a section on the inspector's form to note 'infestations'. Pheasants were noted as 'pests' on many of the farms on the King's estates at Sandringham in Norfolk (MAF 32/735/243).

condition of farm roads and fences, classified as 'good', 'fair', and 'bad'. No rights of way information as such is given. The survey shows the extent of farms at a fixed point in time, the standard and methods of farming in use, who farmed the land and who owned it. A farmer's neighbours can be discovered by looking at the maps for the surrounding farms, then looking them up in the textual records. On a wider scale, one can sometimes form an idea of the interrelationship between local people, particularly the pattern of leasing parcels of land, and grazing rights, perhaps on commons.

Summary

The documents produced for the National Farm Survey can, if you are lucky, take your research back to the First World War or before, to the time of the 1910 Valuation

Office survey of property, or even to the 1901 census and beyond. They are a rich source of detail about land ownership and land usage in mid-twentieth century England and Wales.

Other records

Ministry of Agriculture and Fisheries Divisional Office Records (**MAF 145–149** and **MAF 157–182**) contain some information on both the 1940 and 1941–1943 surveys. In particular, the records for the Oxford division (**MAF 169**) include individual cases of farms taken into the control of the County War Agricultural Executive Committee, as well as records on the ploughing-up of the Berkshire downlands.

MAF 38

Records of the planning and implementation of the two surveys of 1940 and of 1941–3 are contained within the record series **MAF 38**, in the sections **MAF 38/206-217**; **MAF 38/469–473**; and **MAF 38/865–867**. A copy of the 'Revised Instructions for the Completion of Farm Records and Maps', 1941, is in **MAF 38/207**. Instructions for the completion of the 4 June 1941 returns are in **MAF 38/470**.

Summarized reports by county on the 1940 survey are in **MAF 38/213**. No individual farm records of the 1940 survey appear to survive. A proof copy of the *National Farm Survey, England & Wales (1941–1943): a Summary Report* (HMSO, 1946), together with copies of press releases, is in **MAF 38/216**; the summary report contains a statistical analysis of the survey data. Statistical analysis of the National Farm Survey arranged by county is in **MAF 38/852–863**.

MAF 48

Correspondence on land and related matters, with papers of the County War Ags under the sub-heading 'Cultivation of Lands Orders'. There is material on particular cases of land requisitioning, ploughing up, and compulsory purchase.

MAF 65

Parish Lists for June 1941: arranged by county and parish, sometimes with the Lists for June 1940 attached. These provide the full postal address of each farm within the parish, and of the owner (if not the owner/occupier), with statistics of acreages under cultivation. The difference in the area of each holding between 1940 and 1941, and the reason for this, are also given. There is an index to parish numbers in **MAF 65/81**. Please note that these records are closed under the Agriculture Act of 1947.

MAF 68

Parish Summaries of Agricultural Returns: statistics calculated from the yearly census returns, of which the 4 June 1941 returns in the National Farm Survey provide a unique survival. The system of code numbers used is the same for both sets of records.

MAF 80

Minutes of the County War Agricultural Executive Committees, and of their various sub-committees, some volumes of which have detailed indexes that include farm names, are held in **MAF 80**. These records have a closure period of 50 years, and the date of the latest piece is 1972, but they may be seen by readers signing an undertaking form.

Records held elsewhere

An abridged report on the equivalent, but more limited farm survey carried out in Scotland, 1941–3 is in **MAF 38/217**. No individual farm records survive for Scotland, but maps showing farm boundaries are held at the National Archives of Scotland in series RHP 75001–75285. The NAS also holds records of the Scottish Agricultural Executive Committees.

5 How to find an Ordnance Survey sheet number

The Valuation Office maps and the National Farm Survey maps are both series of printed Ordnance Survey maps marked in manuscript to show field and/or farm boundaries and the reference numbers by which individual textual records may be identified. More specific information about the maps as used for the two surveys is given in the appropriate chapter above. This section simply sets out to explain how to use the key sheets which enable you to identify the map sheet relevant to the area in which you are interested.

To find the reference for a Valuation Office map, first consult the County Diagrams (Key Sheets), which are kept in the central map reference cabinet in the Map and Large Document Reading Room. These sheets are reduced photocopies of Ordnance Survey index maps, to which have been added in manuscript information about tithe districts. They were originally used by the Tithe Commission as a guide to the tithe districts created for the administration of the Tithe Commutation Act 1836 (see p. 14), but they also serve as a key to Ordnance Survey sheets at the 1:10,560, 1:2500, and 1:1250 scales. Ignore all the manuscript information for the purposes of the present exercise. You may find a magnifying glass helpful when looking at these sheets, since the background detail can be faint.

The key sheets are in three volumes, arranged in alphabetical order of county name, as follows:

Volume 1: Bedfordshire – Norfolk
Volume 2: Northamptonshire – Yorkshire
Volume 3: Wales: Anglesey – Radnorshire

Note:
- Hampshire is designated Southampton and so is bound between Somerset and Staffordshire.
- The key sheets for **Essex** and **Northumberland** as used by the Tithe Commission do not apply to most of the Valuation Office records because they refer to earlier editions of Ordnance Survey mapping. Instead, you should refer to the photocopies of the index sheets to the New Series maps for these counties, which have been inserted at the appropriate places in the volumes. Only the Essex sheets used in the Barking and Redbridge valuation districts (**IR 121/2** and **IR 121/17** respectively) are from the earlier edition and may be identified from the key sheets annotated by the Tithe Commission.

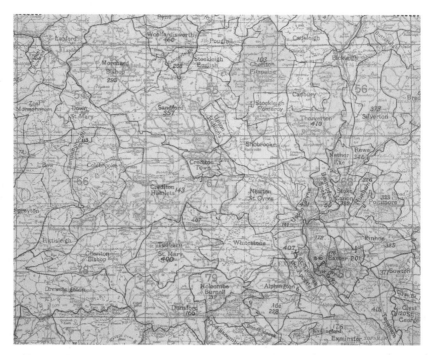

Figure 29a Part of the Ordnance Survey key sheet for Devon: the small red numbers are tithe district numbers.

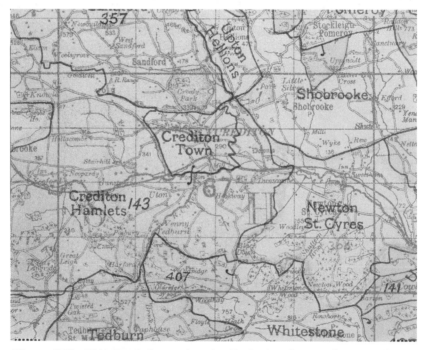

Figure 29b This detail shows that the Ordnance Survey sheet numbers for Crediton town are LXVII.2, LXVII.3, LXVII.6 and LXVII.7 (i.e. 67 converted to a Roman number, followed by the second, third, sixth and seventh of the sixteen smaller sheets into which sheet 67 is divided).

● A further complication for users of the Valuation Office maps occurs in the case of **Tyneside** (north County Durham and south Northumberland), the sheets for which were issued in a separately numbered series. No key sheet to these maps is bound up with the tithe commissioners' set, but one is reproduced in the set of the Ordnance Survey graphic indexes for the 1:2500 and six-inch maps which has been published by David Archer (Newtown, 1991) and is available in the Map and Large Document Reading Room.

Having found the appropriate key sheet, you should proceed as follows:

1. The index sheets have a superimposed grid, which enables you to find the reference to Ordnance Survey sheets at the scales of 1:2500 and six inches to a mile.

2. When you find the right place, note the number in the centre of the large grid rectangle in which your area falls. This is actually the six-inch sheet number for the county.

3. For the **1:2500** maps, there will be 16 sheets covering the area within the numbered grid. The small rectangles representing these sheets are not individually numbered on the index sheet, but once you have found the square in which your property falls, you can mentally number the squares along the rows from 1 in the top left-hand corner to 16 in the bottom right corner. Note this number after the number you already have. This provides the reference **31.15** for the indicated 1:2500 sheet:

1	2	3	4
5	6	7	8
9	10	11	12
13	14	15	16

4. You must now convert the first part of the reference to a Roman numeral (see the leaflet Domestic Records Information 44, *How to Read Roman Numerals*, if you are not familiar with Roman numerals). 31.15 thus becomes **XXXI.15**: this is the Ordnance Survey 1:2500 sheet number for the county in question.

5. For the **1:10,560 (six-inch)** maps, you should again note the number in the centre of the large grid rectangle in which your area falls, but in this case there will be only four sheets covering the area within the numbered grid. These sheets are denoted NW, NE, SW and SE as shown below. The numerical part of the sheet reference must again be converted to a Roman numeral, thus giving a sheet number in the form **XXXI SE**:

6. For the **1:1250** maps, each sheet is equivalent to a quarter of a 1:2500 sheet. So the sheet reference for the same place at the 1:1250 scale is **XXXI.15 SW**:

7. For a **1:500** sheet, the area covered by the corresponding 1:2500 sheet has to be considered as divided into 25 rectangles (five rows of five), each of which represents a sheet at the 1:500 scale (see illustration below). Because of the small scale of the Key Sheets, it is recommended that (where possible) the 1:2500 sheet be ordered first and this used as the key map to identify the 1:500 sheet reference required. The 1:500 sheet indicated has the number **XXXI.15.17**.

1	2	3	4	5
6	7	8	9	10
11	12	13	14	15
16	X 17	18	19	20
21	22	23	24	25

8. A key to the **1:500** map of **Manchester** and **Salford** is available in the Map and Large Document Reading Room.

9. The Ordnance Survey sheets used by the Valuation Office for the **London** area were those mapped at **1:1056** (60 inches to the mile – the so-called 'five-foot plans'). The volume of Key Sheets which serves as an index to this series of maps is kept with the County Diagrams in the central map reference cabinet in the Map and Large Document Reading Room. (Note that there are some London sheets for the Essex border areas at the 1:1250 scale in series **IR 121/17** and **IR 121/20**: no Key Sheet is available for these.)

10. When you have located the place you are seeking on the appropriate Key Sheet, note the reference number at the centre of the rectangle in which it falls, e.g. 10.69. Convert the first part of the reference into a Roman numeral, i.e. **X.69**. This is the London sheet reference that you require (see illustration on p. 92).

11. For some outlying areas of what is now Greater London, it may be necessary to order both the London sheet and that for the appropriate neighbouring county in order to establish which one contains the required Valuation Office information.

12. The London map sheets are in the 19 record series for the Valuation Office London region (**IR 121**). When using the catalogues for these series, always check that you are looking under a 'London' head and at the 1:1056 scale (or, for two London

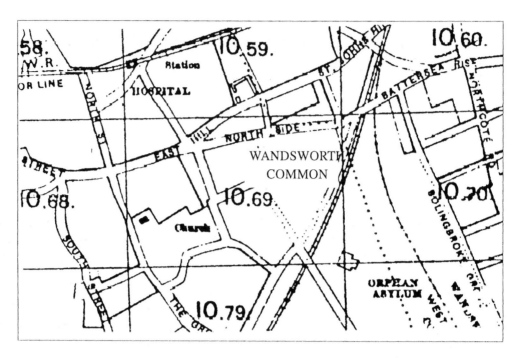

sections in **IR 121/17** and **IR 121/20**, the 1:1250 scale). Sheet X.69 in our example is among the maps transferred from the Merton District Valuation Office (in record series **IR 121/1** – sheet X.69 has the full document reference **IR 121/1/29**).

13. The Ordnance Survey printed the sheet numbers of adjacent sheets in the margins of each map, so if you need to examine an area wider than that shown on the map you are consulting, use these numbers in the margins to obtain the document references for the neighbouring sheets from the online or paper catalogues.

A set of the Ordnance Survey graphic indexes for the 1:2500 and six-inch maps was published as *Ordnance Survey of Great Britain. England and Wales. Indexes to the 1/2500 and 6-Inch Scale Maps* by David Archer (Newtown, 1991) and is available in the Map and Large Document Reading Room. This includes the indexes both to the Old Series and the New Series maps for Essex and Northumberland and to the 1:2500 maps of Tyneside.

6 Case study across the three surveys: Down St Mary, Devon

Rose Mitchell

My grandfather's great-grandfather, Robert May, was a yeoman farmer in this parish in the rural heart of Devon. I knew from the will of his father, also called Robert, that he had inherited a farm there called Merrifield. I decided to trace this property in the tithe, Valuation Office and National Farm surveys.

I looked at the tithe apportionment for Down St Mary (**IR 29/9/160**), which is dated 1842. I first consulted the summary page at the end of the apportionment, and found not only that the elder Robert had owned Merrifield ten years before his death in 1852, but also that he had an interest in two other farms, and that his brother Roger was also farming in this parish.

SUMMARY.

LANDOWNERS.	OCCUPIERS.	TOTAL QUANTITIES. A. R. P.	TOTAL RENT-CHARGE. £. s. d.	LANDOWNERS.	OCCUPIERS.	TOTAL QUANTITIES. A. R. P.	TOTAL RENT-CHARGE. £. s. d.
					Brought forward	917 1 34	130 3 1
Cheriton, Mrs. ..	Tucker, John ..	14 2 2	1 17 0	Shobrooke, William, and			
Cheriton, Joseph, senior, and				Shobrooke, Joseph, (Lessee)	Clement, Abraham	3 2 27	0 11 7
Cheriton, Joseph, junior ..	Themselves	49 1 35	9 5 0	Sturt, H. C., Esquire	Cheriton, Joseph	151 2 23	13 3 5
Cheriton, William	Himself	40 1 29	7 0 0		"	64 0 29	6 1 2
Kellon, John	Himself	81 0 26	13 7 0		Shobrooke, William	92 1 26	12 17 0
May, Robert....	Himself	55 1 2	5 10 2		Kellon, Philip ..	33 0 36	3 18 9
Moon, Thomas..	Himself	2 2 18	0 14 9		Hooper, Mrs. ..	27 3 24	3 3 9
	"	6 2 8	0 11 2		"	61 2 31	6 19 3
	"	78 3 15	9 7 8		May, Robert....	70 0 39	8 0 10
Pope, John, Esquire	Himself	1 2 4	0 0 9		May, Roger	60 0 36	6 15 2
	Snell, John	22 3 27	3 10 0	May, Roger......(Lessee)	"	58 0 34	6 9 3
	"	151 2 26	16 10 0	May, Robert......(Lessee)	Himself	62 1 7	9 15 7
	Brewer, William	11 3 15	1 15 9	Sharland, Richard (Lessee)	Searles, William	48 2 18	8 3 8
	Gribble, John ..	7 1 20	1 2 3	Stell, ...(Lessee)	"	150 0 25	16 18 3
	Hammacott, John	40 0 39	4 12 0	Cheriton, Joseph.. (Lessee)	Himself	1 0 8	0 1 0
	Tucker, John ..	3 0 25	0 11 2	Partridge, Andrew (Lessee)	Himself	135 0 5	10 9 2
Avery, Elizabeth ..(Lessee)	Herself, and Avery, Richard	0 0 34	0 0 7	Tucker, George, Esquire	Hall, Samuel....	31 0 5	2 16 4
Radford, B. T., Esquire	Cheriton, William	224 2 0	40 10 0	Wreford, Samuel, Esquire ..	Moon, Thomas..	58 0 34	6 9 3
	Avery, John, and others	0 2 32	0 0 6	Wreford, John, Esquire	Himself	60 0 32	7 0 0
	Shobrooke, Joseph	119 1 23	13 10 0	Wreford, William, Esquire ..	Himself	62 2 21	7 0 0
	Rice, George....	1 0 29	0 5 6		Waste	6 3 10	
	Dunn, William ..	0 1 30	0 1 0	Radford, Rev. W. T. A. (Glebe)	Himself and another	50 1 5	
	Warren, George and				Public Roads....	33 0 12	
	Clement, Richard	0 2 4	0 0 10		Rivers	16 1 24	
	Carried forward	917 1 34	130 3 1			2229 3 35	265 0 0

Figure 30a The summary page at the end of the apportionment shows Robert May as owner for one farm, owner (lessee) for another farm, and occupier of another farm. It also shows farms owned and occupied by his brother Roger (IR 29/9/160).

The full entry in the schedule of apportionment for Merrifield farm shows Robert (presumably the elder) as owner and occupier, and gives details of each plot number. This shows that Merrifield was an arable farm of just over 55 acres, with two parcels classed as moorland, and a farmhouse. Robert had to pay a tithe rentcharge of £5.10s.2d on this farm.

Owner	Occupier	No.	Name		Use		A R P	£ s d	
							81 0 26	13 7 0	
May, Robert	Himself		**MERRIFIELD.**						
		50	North Merrifield ..	......	Arable	......	7 2 18	0 18 2	A
		51	Barn Close	.. ...	Arable....	......	6 0 37	0 13 0	A
		52	Clover Moor	......	Arable	......	3 2 25	0 7 3	A
		53	House and Lane ..	.....	Buildings & Lane		0 1 35		
		54	Cross Park	......	Arable	......	6 2 20	0 16 9	A
		55	Seven Acres	......	Arable	......	7 1 35	0 18 0	A
		56	Six Acres ...	......	Arable....	......	6 2 0	0 15 9	A
		57	Five Acres ...	.. ...	Arable....	......	5 3 10	0 14 0	A
		58	Great Moor	......	Moor	......	7 2 18	0 4 9	A
		59	Little Moor	......	Moor	......	3 1 4	0 2 6	A
							55 1 2	5 10 2	
Moon, Thomas	Himself		**CUNNETTS.**						
		83	Corner Close	......	Garden ..	......	0 3 33	0 5 5	
		84	Bewdown Close....	......	Arable....	......	1 0 7	0 5 10	A.A.L.
		85	Dallys Mead	......	Garden ..	......	0 2 18	0 3 6	
							2 2 18	0 14 9	

Figure 30b The detailed entry in the apportionment for Robert May's farm of Merrifield.

In his will, Robert the elder specified that his two unmarried daughters were to stay at Merrifield for a year after his death, and could then move out if they wished. He did not mention his wife, as she had died a few months before he made his will. By the time of the 1881 census, the two daughters, still unmarried, were living with their elder, married sister and her family on a nearby farm.

In the tithe file for Down St Mary (**IR 18/1273**) Robert and Roger May are mentioned several times. The tithe collector's report shows the amount of tithe that the Mays had been paying through the 1830s; and the fact that they, like most of the other local farmers, were given an abatement, is evidence that farmers were going through difficult times in the early years of this decade. The file also contains the text of an appeal by a neighbour who thought he had been assessed too harshly by the tithe valuer, and who thought that Robert should have been asked to pay more.

Robert May (again, presumably, the elder) is listed in the tithe apportionment as occupier of another farm, Middle Lammacott. The detailed entry shows this to be a mixed farm of just over 61 acres, with arable, some pasture and orchards, and several copses. There was also some moorland, which may indicate that sheep were kept. There is an entry for 'House, yard and lane', which shows that the lane was privately owned, and the map shows its extent. The 1851 census shows that Robert and his family were then living at this farm.

Robert is also listed as owner (lessee) and occupier of East Lammacott farm, another mixed farm, with a small amount of timber and underwood, which would have been used for fencing and repair work around the farm. There was also a house and garden there.

Robert's younger brother Roger is noted as owner (lessee) on the neighbouring farms of Higher and Lower Lammacott.

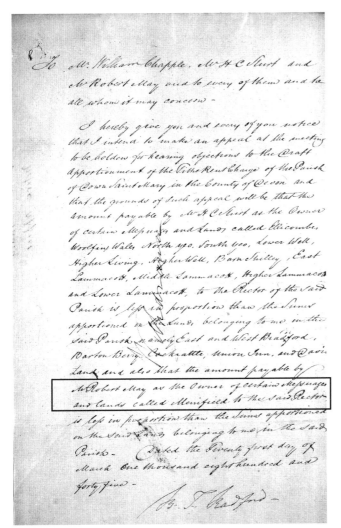

Figure 31 A page from the tithe file for Down St Mary (IR 18/1273), where Robert May is mentioned in a neighbour's appeal against his tithe valuation.

I knew from the 1881 census that Robert the younger and his wife Susan were resident at a farm called Higher Living in the same parish at that time. The original tithe apportionment shows that this farm was not owned by the May family in 1842, but it does provide details of the farm and the house, garden and court, so one can get some idea of the place where Robert and his family later lived. There are a number of altered apportionments for Down St Mary. The first altered apportionment, of 1857, was made to show the line of the North Devon Railway through the parish. The second altered apportionment, of 1867, includes a small plan of Higher Living and parcels to the south, one of which (468b) was now occupied by Robert May, and used as arable. This suggests that Robert and Susan may have moved to Higher Living by this date.

Robert the younger inherited Merrifield in 1852 when he was a young man in his early twenties; he died in 1904, aged 77. I turned to the Valuation Office survey for this area to see what had happened to this property by 1910; the relevant field book (**IR 58/4602**)

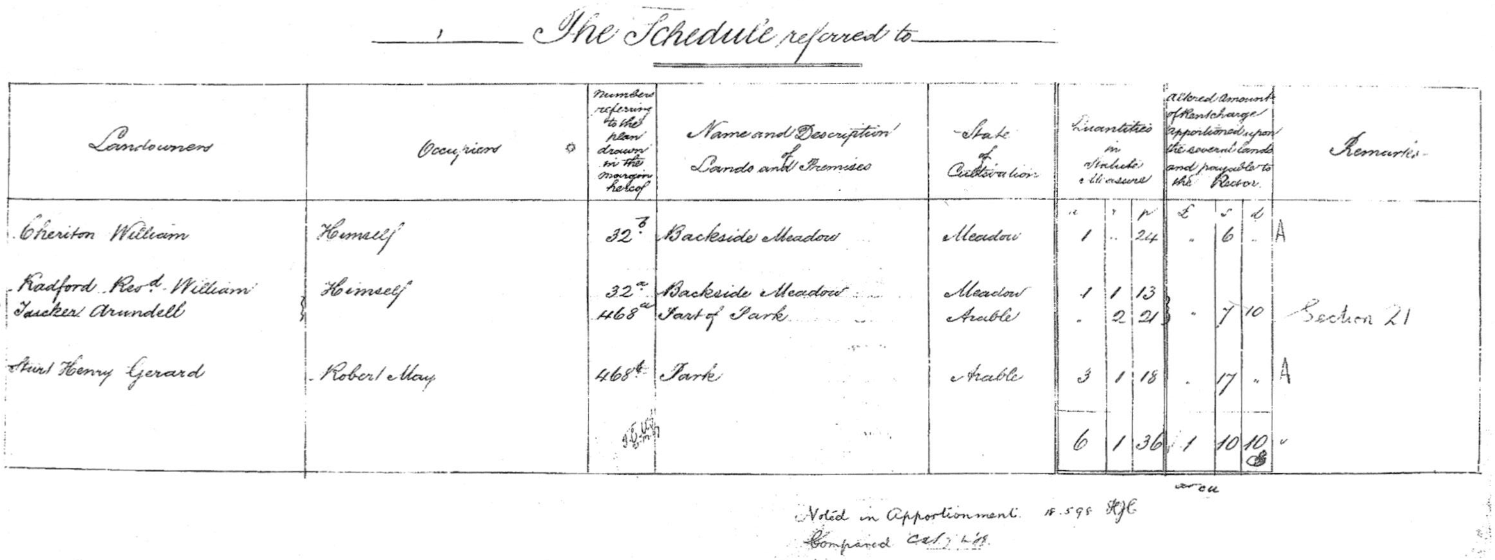

The Schedule referred to

Landowners	Occupiers	Number referring to the plan drawn in the margin hereof	Name and Description of Lands and Premises	State of Cultivation	Quantities in Statute Measure	Altered amount of rentcharge apportioned on the several lands and payable to this Rector	Remarks
Crichton William	Horsey	32a	Backside Meadow	Meadow	1 . 24	£ s d . 6 .	A
Radford Rev.d William Stucleu Arundell	Horsey	32a 468a	Backside Meadow East Park	Meadow Arable	1 1 13 2 21	7 10	Section 21
And Henry Gerard	Robert May	468a	Park	Stable	3 1 18	7 .	A
					6 1 36 1	10 10 .	

Valid in Apportionment n.596 896

Compared Col.2 49.

Figures 32a and 32b An altered apportionment and plan for Down St Mary show Robert May occupying Higher Living in 1867 (IR 29/9/160).

Figure 32b

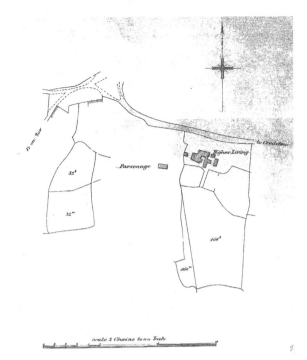

shows that Merrifield (hereditament number 33) was owned by Susan A. May, Robert's
widow, but that she only had a freehold life interest in the farm. It was occupied first by
Anthony Garnish on a lease taken out in Michaelmas 1907, and then by I. W. Squire.

The tithe survey was not concerned with buildings, and the house and farm
buildings at Merrifield were only shown in outline on the tithe map. The Valuation
Office survey was concerned with the value of property, however, which was affected
by how many rooms it had, how well it was built, and its condition. The field book
gives a detailed description and plan of Merrifield (see p. 98). From this we find that
the house was 'old and in fair repair'; that it had five bedrooms, a parlour, dining
room, kitchen, dairy and pantry. There is a note that the water was unfit for drinking,
and an odd note: 'This farm has a very bad approach, is chiefly arable and somewhat
heavy'; presumably this refers to the situation of the farm regarding access roads and
the type of soil. The plan of the farmhouse and buildings has a key to the use of all the
outbuildings. Although the Valuation Office survey was not concerned with details of
livestock, one can infer the type of animals kept from the names of the farm buildings
such as pig house, fowl house, bullock house, calves house and stable.

Susan May died in February 1911. Her eldest son had already died aged 35, leaving
my great-grandfather a fatherless boy of five who does not seemed to have inherited
any of these holdings. Another son of Susan's was working at copper mines a few
miles away rather than farming, according to the 1901 census. A third son had died in
infancy. The field book entry is annotated in a different hand, with a date in
November 1911, to say that the next owners of Merrifield were Mrs Boulter and Mrs
Pearse: these were Susan and Robert's daughters. Thus Merrifield was still 'in the
family', but it was no longer owned by a May.

Includes Ref no 82.

Reference No.

Map. No. LIV. 14. B E H J Q.

Situation *Merrifields + pt Higher Thorne Down St Mary.*

Description *Land with Farm House + buildings*

Extent *65 ac 2 ro.* 60 ac 3 ro *perches*

Gross Value {Land, £
Buildings, £

Rateable Value {Land, £ 32
Buildings, £ 49.

Gross Annual Value, Schedule A, £

Occupier *Anthony Garnish how Mr J W Squire*

Owner *Susan A. May*

Interest of Owner *Life Interest Freehold*

Superior interests *Present owners Mrs Pearn Jubilee Farm St Awlish*
Mrs Boulter Blanche Ho.
Pomphlett
N. Plymouth

Subordinate interests

Occupier's tenancy, Term *10 years* from *Michaelmas 1907*

How determinable *Lease*

Actual (or Estimated) Rent, £ *77*

Any other Consideration paid

Outgoings—Land Tax, £ *none* paid by
Tithe, £ *4 : 10* paid by
Other Outgoings

Who pays (a) Rates and Taxes (b) Insurance *(a) occupier (b) owner*

Who is liable for repairs *Owner*

Fixed Charges, Easements, Common Rights and Restrictions

Former Sales. Dates
Interest

Reference No.

Particulars, description, and notes made on inspection *1st Nov 1911*

Cob & slated Farm House in fair repair containing
5 Bedrooms up. Parlour Kitchen Dining Room Dairy
& larder. Water from pump bad unfit for drinking
purposes. Ord Nos 179 & 180. are now the sole property
of Mrs Boulter. The buildings are old and in
fair repair — This farm has a very bad approach
is chiefly arable & somewhat heavy —

Charges, Easements, and Restrictions affecting market value of Fee Simple

Public path passes across Ord Nos 198 + 202.

Tithes £3. 13. 4 x 25 =   £2 x 25 = £50
                              = £92

Valuation.—Market Value of Fee Simple in possession of whole property in its present condition *Estimated Rental value* £66. 0. 0
Less Repairs *£7. 2. £9. Insurance £1*   10. 0. 0
                                          56. 0. 0
By *22½ years purchase* £1260
Less Tithes   92
               1168
Add Timber   12
               1180   £ 1180

Deduct Market Value of Site under similar circumstances, but if divested of structures, timber, fruit trees, and other things growing on the land   £ 900

Difference Balance, being portion of market value attributable to structures, timber, &c. ....£ 280

Divided as follows :—
Buildings and Structures *£10. 6. 11.3* ......£ 230

Figures 33a and 33b The Valuation Office field book entry for Merrifield (IR 58/4602).

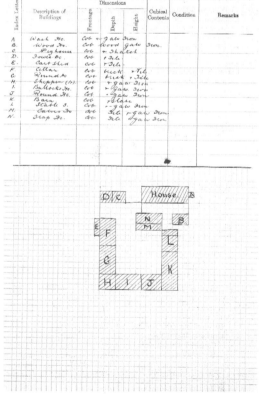

Index Letter	Description of Buildings	Frontage	Depth	Height	Cubical Contents	Condition	Remarks
A	Wash Ho.	Cob &	9 als	Iron			
B	Wood Ho.	Cob	wood	galv	Iron		
C	Pig house	Cob	+	Thatch			
D	Fowls Ho.	Cob	+	Tile			
E	Cart Shed	Cob	+	Tile			
F	Cellar	Cob	brick	+ Tile			
G	Round Ho.	Cob	brick	+ Tile			
H	Shippon (14)	Cob	+	galv	Iron		
J	Bullocks Ho.	Cob	+	galv	Iron		
G	Round Ho.	Cob	+	galv	Iron		
K	Barn	Cob	+	Slate			
L	Stable 3.	Cob	+	galv	Iron		
M	Calves Ho.	Cob	Tile	+ galv	Iron		
N	Trap Ho.	Cob	Tile	& galv	Iron		

Figure 33c Plan of Merrifield with key to buildings (IR 58/4602).

I do not know what then happened to the property between the daughters' ownership in 1911 and 1935, when a Mr Ridd took over the farm. The relevant forms of the National Farm Survey (NFS) for Down St Mary (**MAF 32/666/90**) show that in 1941 it was owned by Mr Hooper, of the Post Office in Zeal Monachorum, and farmed by W. Ridd, who had no family working on the farm, just one worker, and who had been there for six years, i.e. from about 1935.

It is useful to compare the tithe and NFS records for the same farm. The tithe record names the fields, their acreage and uses but does not indicate livestock types or numbers; the NFS gives only overall acreage for different crops rather than naming the fields in which they were grown, but does go into a lot of detail about types, ages and uses of livestock, for instance the number of two-year-old ewes kept for breeding. Using these two sources, it becomes clear that the farm had probably always supported a small flock of sheep; the tithe survey only notes the presence of moorland, but the NFS says that there were 79 sheep in 1941, so putting the two together, it seems possible that there were sheep in 1841, and that they grazed upon the moorland shown on the tithe map. The NFS also shows that the farm in 1941 kept 36 cattle, 6 pigs, 2 horses and 150 poultry, for which a small acreage of corn was grown as feed. There was still no electricity, and water was still drawn from a well for the farmhouse and buildings – one hopes, for Mr Ridd's sake, that the quality of the water had improved in the time since it received adverse comment by the Valuation Office surveyor.

When I checked through the NFS forms for the rest of the parish, I found some grazing used by Mr A. May, next to Higher Living farm where Robert and Susan May had lived with their family in the 1860s to 1880s. It was noted that A. May's main holding was in an adjoining parish, Colebrooke, and that he had farmed there for 11 years, i.e. since 1930. On looking at the NFS forms for Colebrooke, I found that A. May was at Beers Farm, which lies on the parish boundary with Down St Mary, just a few miles from Merrifield Farm. 'A. May' was Albert May, born in 1898 to William May, who is shown at Beers Farm in the Valuation Office survey and whose grandfather John May was noted as farming at Beers in the tithe survey. So the same family had been on this farm in direct line for a hundred years, and Albert's son still farms at Beers today.

My search for the records of one farm, Merrifield, apparently showed that it had gone out of the May family by the Second World War. By checking through all of the National Farm Survey records for the parish, I was able to find another branch of the family, of which I had been unaware. This shows the value of thorough research: it can be disappointing not to find the record you were hoping for, but you may still find unexpected and interesting information.

Even if a family only stayed in a property for a short time, it may still be worth checking the three surveys. They all provide the names of owner and occupier of a property, but otherwise, they each provide different information. The tithe survey provides details of all the plots on a farm, their use and acreage. The Valuation Office survey may tell you what the buildings were like, and if you are lucky, as I was, there may be a plan. The National Farm Survey says which crops were grown and which animals were kept, and how long the farmer had held his farm. Taken together, all this information can give you a valuable insight into how and where people lived across time.

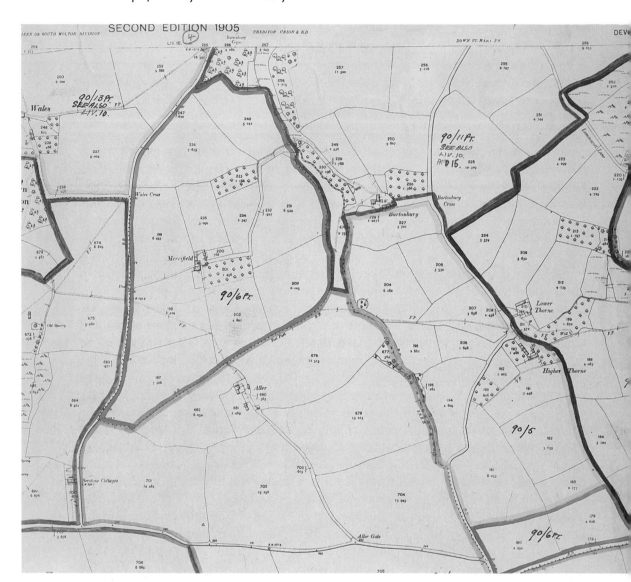

Figure 34 The National Farm Survey map which shows Merrifield is Ordnance Survey Devon sheet LIV.14 (MAF 73/10/54): this gives the number of the farm (90/6) and shows the farm buildings in the centre of fields, with an access lane, several areas of wood, and a footpath running across the south-west of the farm. 'Pt' after the farm number shows that part of the farm lay elsewhere; in this case, two fields belonging to Merrifield Farm are shown at the lower right, with Aller Farm lying between the two.

7 Case study across the three surveys: Darlaston, Staffordshire

Geraldine Beech

My great-great-grandfather, Richard Rose, born probably in 1827, was a manufacturer of nuts and bolts in Darlaston, Staffordshire. Already at the time of the tithe survey, Darlaston was a highly industrial area, with a population (in 1841) of over 6,000 people. Communications in this booming area of the Midlands were good: the tithe map (**IR 30/32/78**) made in 1842 shows roads, the Birmingham Canal and towpath, and the Grand Junction Railway. The apportionment (**IR 29/32/78**) identifies a number of pieces of land as belonging to the Birmingham Coal Company.

The tithe file (**IR 18/9333**) contains much information about the town and its immediate surroundings and is of interest to local historians as well as to genealogists for the light it throws on the environment of those who lived there. In contrast to information in the apportionment about the principal landowners and the semi-rural outskirts of the town, the tithe file contains details from which we can build up a picture of an impoverished and overcrowded community. The rector reported to the assistant tithe commissioner in December 1839 that there were 1,500 houses in the parish: 'Most of these are of a miserable description and occupied, principally, by poor persons employed in the Coal, Iron and Mines and Works. . . . In some Houses (most of them miserable Habitations) . . . there were 15 persons.' The impact of industrialization on the landscape is clear: 'There is a good deal of what is called "Waste Bank" – land thrown out of cultivation and perfectly useless, owing to the refuse thrown from the Pitts and Works.' A later report reinforces the point: 'The surface is much covered by the refuse of the Coal and Iron Mines, and damaged by the lawless trespass of the numerous population.' For the landowners, it was the minerals rather than any agricultural potential which were to be exploited: in October 1842, the assistant tithe commissioner reported, 'A large part of the surface is the property, and in the occupation of Iron Masters, who regard the Minerals underneath it, but are very indifferent as to its rural produce.' And this despite the fact that the large number of horses required to work in the mines 'must give a high value to all green produce'.

Fifty acres in the centre of the town (where most of the population lived) were no longer titheable: the assistant tithe commissioner's preliminary report following his visit on 4 December 1839 deducted almost £13,000 for houses and other non-titheable property from the total parish assessment of £14,600. This non-titheable area was not surveyed for the Tithe Commission and is not shown on the tithe map. There is no mention of Richard Rose or his family in the tithe apportionment, although the apportionment does identify a number of manufactories, quarries, 'mine waste' and other industrial sites. The map originally intended to be used for the tithe survey had been made in 1833 and was described by the assistant commissioner as 'extremely defective and inaccurate'. In the event, a new map appears to have been made in 1842: it shows that even in such an industrialized area, open countryside was not far away. The straggling Darlaston Brook still meandered alongside the canal. Much of the land was still unenclosed, and the map clearly shows the open fields and strips which must have remained unchanged since medieval times. One consequence of this was the difficulty of establishing the boundaries of individual landowners' holdings.

Richard Rose clearly prospered: his estate when he died in 1870 was valued at £877 17s 11d, a very substantial sum at that time. His will bequeathed all his personal estate to his wife, Hannah, and indicates that his brother and business partner, James Rose, owed him £800. The 1871 census lists James Rose as a bolt, nut and latch maker, employing 20 men, 12 girls and 7 boys.

By the time of the 1881 census, the widowed Hannah Rose was living in Willenhall Street, Darlaston. By then, her daughter, Sarah, had left home, having married Joseph Beech, my father's grandfather. The 1881 census also lists Richard Rose's brother and partner, James Rose, now aged 55. Business had obviously continued to flourish: James is described as a bolt and screw manufacturer employing 90 hands; and also as a licensed victualler.

By 1901, the family had moved from Staffordshire to Manchester, but family lore states that my great-grandmother, Sarah Beech, continued to receive a regular weekly payment from the Rose firm until her death in 1902.

I thought it might be interesting to see whether there was any reference to the Rose firm in the Valuation Office survey. I proceeded on the basis of the one address I knew: Willenhall Street, Darlaston.

The relevant OS 1:2500 sheet is Staffordshire LXIII.13 (**IR 129/7/31**): I established this by using the key sheets (see Chapter 5). However, most of the area of this map is unannotated with hereditament numbers, and the density of buildings suggests that the area might have been mapped at a larger scale. The catalogue for **IR 129/7** does indeed describe maps at 1:1250. Four sheets at a scale of 1:1250 are needed to show the same area as one sheet at a scale of 1:2500. For sheet LXIII.13, the equivalent sheets at 1:1250 are sheets LXIII.13 NW, LXIII.13 NE, LXIII.13 SW and LXIII.13 SE. Willenhall lies north-west of Darlaston, and examination of the 1:2500 sheet indicated that the area around Willenhall Street was indeed likely to be shown on the north-west sheet (i.e. the upper left quarter): I therefore looked at sheet LXIII.13 NW (**IR 129/7/77**) and duly found Willenhall Street.

My eye was immediately drawn to a large plot just round the corner in Baulk Lane designated on the Ordnance Survey map as 'London Works (Bolt & Nut)'. This was identified as hereditament number 1135. The houses in Willenhall Street, mostly small and terraced, bore hereditament numbers in the 1800s and 1900s.

The Ordnance Survey map was printed in 1912, and red ink additions show numerous hereditaments which are not on the printed map. This indicates that even between the time of the latest Ordnance Survey and the Valuation Office survey, extensive development had taken place.

I then looked for the field books for Darlaston. The books for Darlaston are easy to identify because Darlaston was itself an income tax parish. So an online search under 'Darlaston', limited to record series **IR 58**, rapidly identified all the relevant field books. This led to **IR 58/86922** (for hereditament 1135), **IR 58/86929** (for hereditament numbers 1801–1900) and **IR 58/86930** (for hereditament numbers 1901–2000).

- **IR 58/86922**, entry no 1135, relates to bolt and nut works, offices, land, etc. belonging to James & Richard Rose Ltd and situated in Baulk Lane, Darlaston. However, when I turned over the page, I found that entry no 1136 also relates to property owned by James & Richard Rose Ltd. This is described as 'principally land used as a tip for spoil with pool the water from which is used for boilers etc at adjoining works'. A small, rough plan shows the position of hereditament 1136 and also of hereditament 4013. I had barely noticed the latter on the Ordnance Survey map.

This led me to:

- **IR 58/86951**, entry no 4013, which is described as 'land fronting Willenhall Street, being an accommodation Road'. The assessment in respect of this plot was clearly deducted from that in respect of hereditament 1136.
- **IR 58/86929**, entry no 1833, relates to stabling and premises in Willenhall Street belonging to James & Richard Rose Ltd, London Works, Darlaston. As if more confirmation were needed, a note states, 'Valued with Darlaston 1135'.
- **IR 58/86930** entry no 1917 relates to a shop and warehouse in Willenhall Street belonging to J. & R. Rose. I infer from a note in the entry that the shop had been demolished by 1914.

So the firm was clearly still in existence and thriving at the time of the Valuation Office survey. This is interesting, because Richard had died in 1870 and James was apparently dead by 1901 – he does not appear at all in the census for that year. Richard Rose had a son, also Richard, who may well be the Richard Rose named in **IR 58/86929** as owner of the works.

Entries 1135 and 1136 indicate that the lands to which they relate were subject to tithe payments. Since I failed to identify such lands on the tithe map, I looked at the district record map (**IR 90/32/78**) made following the Tithe Act 1936. This led me to discover that the lands occupied by the London works were tithe plot numbers 320 and 323. The tithe apportionment and map then showed that these lands were in 1842 part of an area known as Radley Gutter – grassland with no buildings at all on them.

The Valuation Office records show that Darlaston had expanded enormously. The tithe records suggest that there was probably a maximum of 2,500 units of property in 1840; by the time of the Valuation Office survey, this had swollen to 4,095 hereditaments.

Because of the very industrial nature of Darlaston, I was surprised to find that there are any National Farm Survey records at all. The map (sheet LXIII.13 in **MAF 73/37/63**)

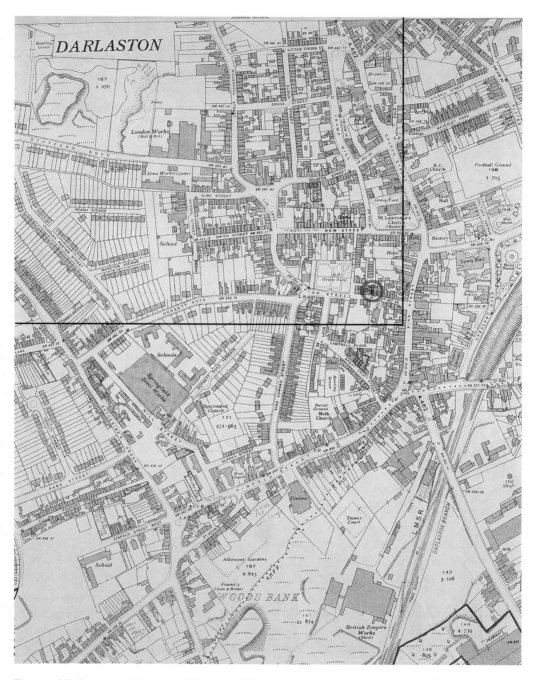

Figure 35 Part of a Valuation Office 1:2,500 scale map of Darlaston, Staffordshire (IR 129/7/31). Note that, because of the density of building, much of the map is not annotated to show hereditament numbers – these should be sought on a larger-scale map of the area.

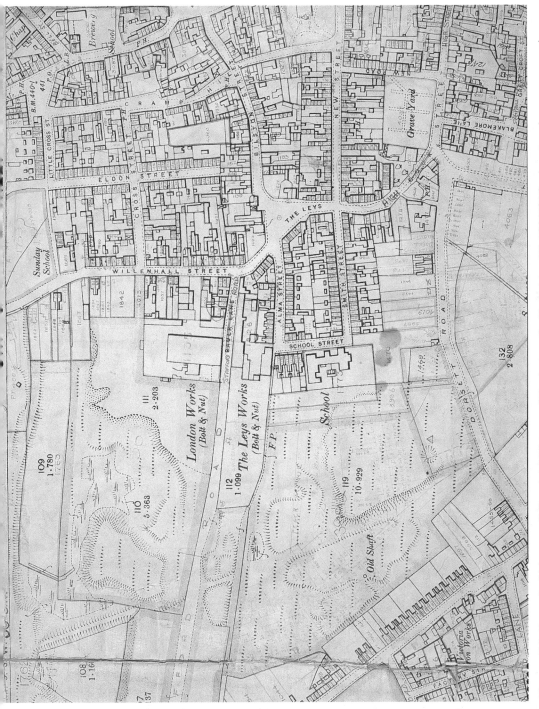

Figure 36 Part of a Valuation Office 1:1,250 map of Darlaston, Staffordshire (IR 129/7/77), showing the area around Willenhall Street. The London Works at the corner of Willenhall Street and Baulk Lane are identifiable as hereditament number 1135.

Left form (top)

...11.35...Reference No.   Map. No. 370

Situation *Gaulk Lane*

Description *Bolts Nut Works, Offices, land &c*

Extent

Gross Value { Land £ / Buildings £ } *3294*   Rateable Value { Land £ / Buildings £ } *207/10*

Gross Annual Value, Schedule A, £

Occupier } *James & Richard Rose Ltd*

Owner } *London Works Darlaston.*

Interest of Owner *Freehold*

Superior interests

Subordinate interests

Occupier's tenancy, Term   from

How determinable

Actual (or Estimated) Rent, £

Any other Consideration paid

Outgoings—Land Tax, £   paid by

Tithe, £ *12/4*   paid by

Other Outgoings

Who pays (a) Rates and Taxes (b) Insurance } *owners.*

Who is liable for repairs

Fixed Charges, Easements, Common Rights and Restrictions

Former Sales. Dates *Sep 1892*   *10th Oct 1900* } also

Interest *5790 syds*   *7 yusyyds* } see

Consideration *£9620*   *£4* } £ IV.

Subsequent Expenditure

Owner's Estimate. Gross Value

Full Site Value

Total Value

Assessable Site Value

Site Value Deductions claimed

Roads and Sewers. Dates of Expenditure / Amounts

Right form (top)

Reference No.

Particulars, description, and notes made on inspection

See File.

Charges, Easements, and Restrictions affecting market value of Fee Simple

Valuation.—Market Value of Fee Simple in possession of whole property in its present condition

Bldgs 3934
Mchy 935
Land 303
5742
Area 5864 ® Less Tithe 36   £ 5136

Deduct Market Value of Site under similar circumstances, but if divested of structures, timber, fruit trees, and other things growing on the land

@ £250 per acre less tithe £   £ 264

Difference Balance, being portion of market value attributable to structures, timber, &c.   4869

Divided as follows:—

Buildings and Structures...................£ 3934

Machinery ....£ 935

Timber ....£

Fruit Trees ....£

Other things growing on land ....£

Market Value of Fee Simple of Whole in its present condition (as before)   £ 5136

Add for Additional Value represented by any of the following for which any deduction may have been made when arriving at Market Value:—

Charges (excluding Land Tax) Tithes £ 36

Restrictions...................£   £ 36

GROSS VALUE...£ 5172

29 DEC. 1913

Left form (bottom)

...11.36...Reference No.   Map. No. 370

Situation *Gaulk Lane*

Description *Land*

Extent *7:3:18 (? part of this are sold)*

Gross Value { Land £ 87/- / Buildings £ }   Rateable Value { Land £ 7/17 / Buildings £ }

Gross Annual Value, Schedule A, £

Occupier } *James & Richard Rose Ltd, London Works*

Owner } *Darlaston.*

Interest of Owner *Freehold*

Superior interests

Subordinate interests

Occupier's tenancy, Term   from

How determinable

Actual (or Estimated) Rent, £

Any other Consideration paid

Outgoings—Land Tax, £   paid by

Tithe, £ *1:8:2*   paid by

Other Outgoings

Who pays (a) Rates and Taxes (b) Insurance

Who is liable for repairs

Fixed Charges, Easements, Common Rights and Restrictions

Former Sales. Dates *23rd June 1893.*

Interest *Freehold*

Consideration *£200*

Subsequent Expenditure

Owner's Estimate. Gross Value

Full Site Value

Total Value

Assessable Site Value

Site Value Deductions claimed

Roads and Sewers. Dates of Expenditure / Amounts

Right form (bottom)

Reference No.

Particulars, description, and notes made on inspection

Principall Land used as tip for spoil with pool, the water from which is used for boilers at Alsonny works Small piece with frontage to Wellenhall Street. see 4013.

Charges, Easements, and Restrictions affecting market value of Fee Simple

Valuation.—Market Value of Fee Simple in possession of whole property in its present condition

Plot fronting Willenhall St. 833 syds @ 4/- = 40
Back Land 7:1:37 @ £20 = 150
(Less Tithe £1:8:2 × 254 P. = 35.)   150
Amended 9/1/13.   190   35 Tithe
Deduct Market Value of Site under similar circumstances, but if divested of structures, timber, fruit trees, and other things growing on the land   115

as above   155   115

Difference Balance, being portion of market value attributable to structures, timber, &c. ....£   —

Divided as follows:—

Buildings and Structures...................£

Machinery ....£

Timber ....£

Fruit Trees ....£

Other things growing on land ....£

Market Value of Fee Simple of Whole in its present condition (as before)   £ 155   115

Add for Additional Value represented by any of the following for which any deduction may have been made when arriving at Market Value:—

Charges (excluding Land Tax) Tithe £ 35

Restrictions...................£   £ 35

GROSS VALUE...£ 190 150

17 JAN 1913   -7 Oct. 1913

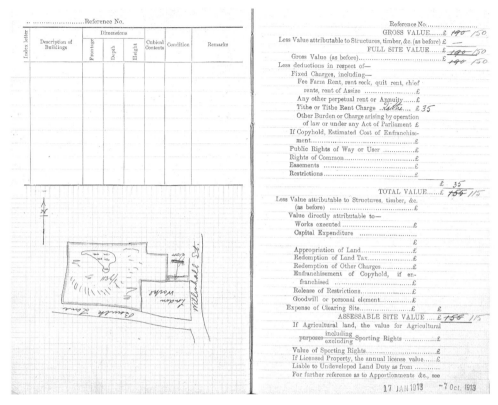

Figure 37a The Valuation Office field book entry for the London Works owned by James and Richard Rose (IR 58/86922, no. 1135). (*See opposite above.*)

Figure 37b The Valuation Office field book entry for the land adjacent to the London Works shows that this was used as a 'tip for spoil' (IR 58/86922, no. 1136). (*See opposite below.*)

Figure 37c A rough plan in the field book entry for hereditament 1136 (IR 58/86922) indicates an access from the street to this land, designated '4013'. The field book entry for hereditament 4013 is IR 58/86951.

bears scarcely a single annotation. Farm records **(MAF 32/591/176)** proved to exist for only two properties in the town. Both relate to poor pasture land, one of ten acres and the other of six and a half acres, all the soil of which is described as 'naturally bad'. Between them, these two pieces of land supported 31 fowl, 5 ducks and 4 horses. There was no electricity, no motive power, no workers were employed, yet the management in both cases was rated 'A': it was evidently recognized that no better use could be made of the available land. Darlaston's contribution to the war effort was clearly not agricultural or horticultural, but through its mines and factories.

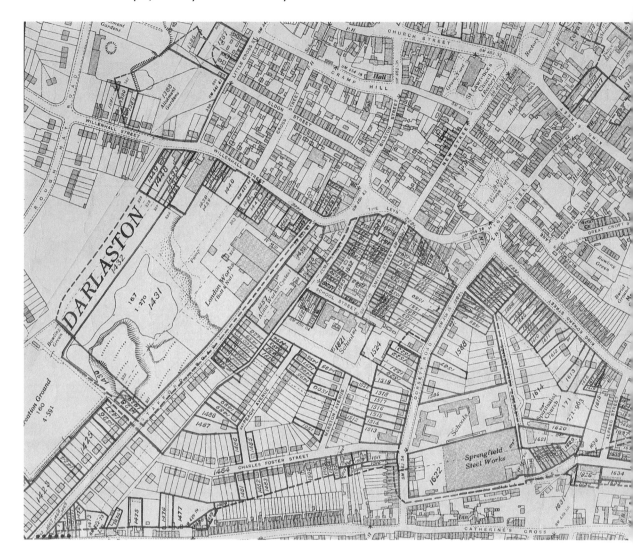

Figure 38 Part of the Tithe Redemption Commission district record map of Darlaston (IR 90/32/78), from which it is possible to establish that the site of the London Works was depicted on the original tithe map as plots 320 and 323. (See also Figure 36, p. 105.)

Figure 39 Detail of the tithe map of Darlaston (IR 30/32/78), showing tithe plots 320 and 323, the land on which the Rose brothers' bolt and nut works were later built. (*See opposite above.*)

Figure 40 Page of the tithe apportionment for Darlaston (IR 29/32/78), showing the entries relating to plots 320 and 323 in Radley Gutter. (*See opposite below.*)

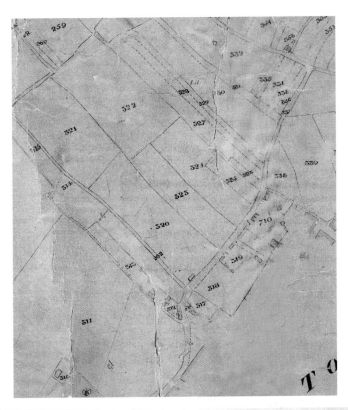

LANDOWNERS.	OCCUPIERS.	Number referring to the Plan.	NAME AND DESCRIPTION of LANDS AND PREMISES.	STATE of CULTIVATION.	QUANTITIES in STATUTE MEASURE.			Amount of Rent-Charge apportioned upon the several Lands, and Payable to *the Rector*		REMARKS.
Charles Adams Esq.ᵉ	Himself	277	Pinfold Street	Ley	1	3	32	16	7	R.33224
		286	do	Garden			30	1	6	N.o.357
	William Brevitt	992	Broad Bridge Piece	Arable	3	1	6	17	0	A.A.I.
	Joseph Butler	186	Wolverhampton Lane	"	2	2	35	17	0	N
		193	do	"		2	29	16	8	N
	Joseph Cockram	67	Heathfield	"		3	23	8	1	N
		65	do	"		3	27	9	6	N
	William Duffield	315	The Leys	Grass		3	18			N
	Samuel Eaton	200	Wolverhampton Lane	Arable		1	29	11	6	N
		201	do	"	1	2	35	16	6	N
	Jacob Forster	177	Meadow north of Canal	Grass		3	35	5	6	N
		177ᵃ	Blakemores Cow Pasture	"			9⅝			N
	Joseph Gibbons	179	Blakemores Cow Pasture	Arable	1	2	30	4	2	N
		182	do	"	1	3	30	7	1	N
		189	do	"	1	1	30			N
	Nehemiah Harper	320	Radley Gutter	Grass	2	1	24	13	4	N
		321	do	"	2	1	2	12	7	N
		322	do	"	2	0	18	16	7	N
	Robert Hartstone	619	Goldings Flat	"	2	3	34	3	0	N
	Mary Hoton	191	Wolverhampton Lane	"	2	3	22	13	0	N
	Jabez Rubery	323	Radley Gutter	"	1	1	18	7	5	N
	Thomas Tisall	324	Radley Gutter	"	1	3	39	8	4	N
	James Underwood	276	Pinfold Street	Arable	1	3	11	15	1	R.33224.
	Thomas Webb	388	Bacon Piece	"				17	0	R.15036.
					37	0	28	13	16	3
Joseph Adams	John Turner	613	Beggars Bridge Piece	Grass	2	3	23	16	3	N
Edward Addenbrooke Addenbrooke and Smith and Charles Riacock	Themselves	234	Rough Hay	Arable	2	0	24	17	11	
		240	do	Brick field				16		
		241ᵃ	do	Mine Waste &c	3	0	16	16	0	A.A.I.
		242	do	Arable	1	2	7	13	11	
		302	In Blakemores Piece	Grass	4	0		19	9	
		410	Long Bridge Piece	Canal Bank			3		6	N
		410	do	Grass			20⅝			
	George Bayley	213	Rough Hay	Arable	1	2	2	13	7	
		214	do	"	1	1	2½	13	7	R.15036.
		339	do	"	1	1	23	13	8	
		360	do	Grass	2	0	35	13	8	A.A.I.
		337	do	"	1	1	32	6	6	
		390	do	"	2	1	31	15	10	
			carried forward		91	2	25⅝	7	1	6

No. 4.—Lavson : Printed and Published (by Authority) by G. ROUTLEDGE, 11, Ryder's Court, Leicester Square.

Further reading

Tithes

G. L. Beech, 'Tithe Maps', *The Map Collector*, no 33, December 1985, pp. 20–25

R. Davies, *The Tithe Maps of Wales* (Aberystwyth, The National Library of Wales, 1999)

E. J. Evans, *The Contentious Tithe: The Tithe Problem and English Agriculture, 1750–1850* (London, Routledge & Kegan Paul, 1976)

R. J. P. Kain, *An Atlas and Index of the Tithe Files of Mid-Nineteenth Century England and Wales* (Cambridge University Press, 1986)

R. J. P. Kain and R. R. Oliver, *The Tithe Maps of England and Wales* (Cambridge University Press, 1995)

R. J. P. Kain and H. C. Prince, *The Tithe Surveys of England and Wales* (Cambridge University Press, 1985)

R. J. P. Kain and H. C. Prince, *Tithe Surveys for Historians* (Chichester, Phillimore, 2000)

M. Sill, 'Using the Tithe Files: A County Durham Study', *The Local Historian*, VII, no 4, November 1986

Valuation Office

B. Short, *The Geography of England and Wales in 1910: An Evaluation of Lloyd George's 'Domesday' of Landownership* (Historical Geography Research Series, no. 22, 1989)

B. Short, 'Local Demographic Studies of Edwardian England and Wales: The Use of the Lloyd George "Domesday" of Landownership', *Local Population Studies*, LI, Autumn 1993, pp. 62–72

B. Short and M. Reed, *Landownership and Society in Edwardian England and Wales: The Finance (1909–10) Act 1910 Records* (University of Sussex, 1987)

B. Short, M. Reed and W. Caudwell, 'The County of Sussex in 1910: Sources for a New Analysis', *Sussex Archaeological Collections*, CXXV, 1987, pp. 199–224

National Farm Survey

P. S. Barnwell, 'The National Farm Survey 1941–1943', *Journal of the Historic Farm Buildings Group*, VII, 1994, pp. 12–19

A. J. H. Jackson, 'The 1941–1943 National Farm Survey: Investigating the Powderham Estate', *Devon and Cornwall Notes and Queries*, Spring 2001, vol. XXXVIII, part IX

R. Mitchell, 'The National Farm Survey', *Ancestors*, Issue 7, April/May 2002

B. Short, C. Watkins, W. Foot and P. Kinsman, *The National Farm Survey 1941–1943: State Surveillance and the Countryside in England and Wales in the Second World War* (Wallingford, CABI Publishing, 1999)

Ordnance Survey maps

J. B. Harley, *Ordnance Survey Maps: A Descriptive Manual* (Southampton, Ordnance Survey, 1975)

R. Hellyer, *Ordnance Survey Small-Scale Maps: Indexes: 1801–1998* (Kerry, David Archer, 1999)

R. Oliver, *Ordnance Survey Maps: A Concise Guide for Historians* (London, Charles Close Society, 1993)

Ordnance Survey of Great Britain. England and Wales. Indexes to the 1/2500 and 6-Inch Scale Maps (Newtown, David Archer, 1991)

Published facsimiles

The Old Series Ordnance Survey Maps of England and Wales: 8 vols (Lympne, Harry Margary, 1975–1991)

Many early large-scale Ordnance Survey maps have been reproduced by Alan Godfrey, Newcastle upon Tyne.

The London Topographical Society has published a number of facsimiles of maps of London; many other local history and archaeological societies have published reproductions of maps of the areas in which they are interested.

General

N. Barratt, *Tracing the History of Your House* (Public Record Office, 2001)

A. Bevan, *Tracing Your Ancestors in the Public Record Office* (6th edn, Public Record Office, 2002)

J. Chapman, *A Guide to Parliamentary Enclosures in Wales* (1992)

C. Delano-Smith and R. J. P. Kain, *English Maps: A History* (The British Library, 1999)

P. Hindle, *Maps for Local History* (London, Batsford, 1988)

C. Sinclair, *Tracing Scottish Local History: A Guide to Local History Research in the Scottish Record Office* (Edinburgh, Her Majesty's Stationery Office, 1994)

D. Smith, *Maps and Plans For the Local Historian and Collector* (London, Batsford, 1988)

W. E. Tate, *A Domesday of English Enclosure Acts and Awards* (Reading, 1978)

J. A. Yelling, *Common Fields and Enclosure in England* (London, Macmillan, 1977)

Index

Italic page numbers refer to illustrations.

Abbey Farm, Muchelney, Somerset, *76–7*
Admiralty
    estate plans, 5
    Form 4-Land, 66, *68*
Admiralty Works Department maps, 7
agricultural depression, 13, 14
Ainderby Quernhow, North Yorkshire, *37*, *39*, *41*
Air Ministry Estates Branch maps, 7
Air Ministry files, 7
air raids, 7
Alphabetical List of Parishes and Places in England and Wales, 55
altered tithe apportionments, 15, 26–8, 95, *96*
    Down St Mary case study, 95, *96*
American Loyalists Claims Commission, 9
annotations, tithe apportionments, 26, 27
appeals
    tithe valuation, 94, 95, *95*
    Valuation Office survey, 67
appropriators, 29
architectural drawings, 9–10
aristocratic tithe owners, 29
armed services, 7
Army: Unit War Diaries, 7
assessable site value, 58
assistant tithe commissioners, 15, 31

Beers Farm, Down St Mary case study, 99
Berkshire downlands ploughing, 85
Birmingham Canal, 101
Birmingham Coal Company, 101
Boconnoc, Cornwall, tithe map, *33*
Bomb Census maps, 7
boundaries
    enclosure award maps, 4
    income tax parishes, 42–3
    national boundaries, 6
    township boundaries, 34
Boundary Awards, 34
Bradford on Avon, Wiltshire, 14
bridleways
    tithe surveys, 35
    Valuation Office survey, 63
Brighton, Sussex, bandstand, *9*
British colonies, 7
British Transport Historical Records, 6–7

Brontë, Reverend Patrick, 29
buildings, 9–10
    tithe surveys, 34

case studies
    Darlaston, Staffordshire, 101–9
    Down St Mary, Devon, 93–100
census returns
    farm, 75
    population, 11, 94, 102
Chatham, Kent, 68
Chatsworth House, Derbyshire 59, *59*
Church, tithe ownership, 13
church buildings, 62
Clannaborough, Devon, Valuation Office survey, *63*
Colebrooke, Down St Mary case study, 99
colleges, tithe ownership, 29
Colonial Office maps, 2
community details
    National Farm Survey, 83–4
    Valuation Office survey, 61–3
commutation, tithes, 13–14
compulsory redemption of tithe rentcharge, 27
corn rent annuity, 27
county boundaries, 6
County Diagrams (Key Sheets), 23, 87–92
county maps, 6–7
County War Agricultural Executive Committees ('County War Ags'), 69, 85, 86
Court of Chancery, 4
Court of Common Pleas, 4
Cranbrook, Kent, 81
Crediton, Devon, *88*
Crop Reporters, 70
crops
    National Farm Survey, 75, 83
    tithe surveys, 32
Crown Estate Commissioners, 4
'Cultivation of Lands Orders', 85

Darlaston, Staffordshire, case study, 101–9
Dawson, Lieutenant Robert K., 18
Derwentwater, 3rd Earl of, 5
Devon, *63*, *82*, *88*, 93–100
Devonshire, Duke of, 59
district record maps (IR 90), 22

districts
tithe survey, 16–17, 23, 28
Valuation Office survey, 38, 44–5
Domesday Books *see* Valuation Books
Down St Mary, Devon, case study, 93–100
Droylesden tithe map, *24*
Duchy of Lancaster, 4, 5

Earl of Derwentwater (3rd), 5
East Florida Claims Commission, 9
ecclesiastical buildings, 62
ecclesiastical tithe ownership, 29
Ellerton, East Riding of Yorkshire, *65*
Enclosure Acts, 13
enclosure award maps, 4
Enfield, Middlesex, *56*
engineering drawings, 9–10
Essex, Ordnance Survey key sheets, 87
estate plans, 4–5
executors, 59

farm codes (NFS), 71, 78
farm conditions, 83
farmers
assessment, 75, 79–80
farming practices, 83
field books, Valuation Office survey (IR 58), 38,
55–8
Darlaston case study, 103, *106–7*
Down St Mary case study, 95, 97–8, *98*
field boundaries, 32
field names, 32
Finance (1909–1910) Act 1910, 36
Finance Act 1920, 37
First World War, 7
first-class tithe maps, 19–20, *19*
five-foot plans, London, 6, 91
Flixton, Lancashire, *19*
food shortages, 69
footpaths
tithe surveys, 35
Valuation Office survey, 63
Foreign Office maps, 2
Forestry Commission, Form 4-Land, 66
Forestry Commissioners, estate plans, 4
Form 4-Land, 38, 66, *68*
Form 36-Land, 66
Form 37-Land, 66
Form 76-Land (mineral rights), 67
Form 77-Land (notice of appeal), 67
full site value, 58

glebe lands, 32, 34
Grand Junction Railway, 101
Greenwich Hospital northern estates, 5
gross value, Valuation Office survey, 57

Hampshire
Ordnance Survey key sheets, 87
tithe nomenclature, 16
Haworth tithe apportionment, *29*
hedges, 32
hereditaments, Valuation Office survey, 38
field books, 58
record maps, 42
Valuation Books, 64
Howe Farm, Ainderby Quernhow, *39*

impropriators, 29
income tax parishes (ITPs), 38
boundaries, 42–3
field books, 55, 57
Valuation Books, 64
increment value duty, 58
calculation, 67
Finance (1909–1910) Act 1910, 36–7
index sheets, National Farm Survey maps, 71–2
Industrial Revolution, 11
industrialization, 13, 101–2
infestations (pests), 84
Inland Revenue Solicitor reports, 67
inspectors, National Farm Survey, 75
ITPs *see* income tax parishes
IR 18 *see* tithe files
IR 29 *see* tithe apportionments
IR 30 *see* tithe maps
IR 58 *see* field books
IR 77 *see* tithe maps supplementary
IR 90 *see* district record maps
Ireland, 18

Jamaica, 8

Kew, Surrey, *72*
key sheets, Ordnance Survey, 23, 87–92
Kipling, Rudyard, 60

land grant maps, 7, 9
Land Revenue Record Office, 4, 6
land use, tithe surveys, 25, 32
Land Value Reference Committee records, 67
landowners
Form 37-Land, 66
tithe apportionments, 25
tithe surveys, 30
Valuation Office survey, 61
landscape features, 33–4
leaflets, 2–3
Leman Street, London, *62*
Lincolnshire, MAF 73 series list, 73, 74
livestock
Down St Mary case study, 99
tithe surveys, 32
living conditions

Darlaston case study, 101
National Farm Survey, 83
tithe survey, 30
Valuation Office survey, 60–61
Llanfihangel, Merionethshire, *20–21*
Lloyd George, David, 36
Lloyd George survey *see* Valuation Office
  survey
local government boundaries, 6
local record offices, 10, 18
local studies libraries, 10
local tithe agents, 31
London
  county and town maps, 7
  five-foot plan, 6, 91
  MAF 73 series list, 74
  Ordnance Survey sheets, 91–2

MAF 32 (National Farm Survey textual
  records), 75–8
MAF 38 (reports and instructions), 85, 86
MAF 48 (correspondence), 85
MAF 65 (Parish Lists), 85
MAF 68 (Parish Summaries), 86
MAF 73 (National Farm Survey maps), 71–4
MAF 80 (County War Agricultural Committee
  minutes), 86
mapmakers, 10, 30–31
Maps and Plans in the Public Record Office, 3
May family, Down St Mary case study, 93–9
mergers (tithe), 27
Merrifield, Down St Mary case study, 93–100
military maps, 7
mineral field books, 61
Ministry of Agriculture, enclosure award
  maps, 4
Ministry of Agriculture and Fisheries
  Divisional Office Records, 85
Ministry of Housing and Local Government, 9
monetary payments, tithes, 13–14
Monmouthshire, 16
moorland, 33
Muchelney, Somerset, *76–7*
Municipal and Parliamentary Boundaries
  Commission, 6

*National Farm Survey, England and Wales
  (1941–1943): A Summary Report* (HMSO,
  1946), 85
National Farm Survey (NFS), 69–86
  Darlaston case study, 103, 107
  Down St Mary case study, 99–100, *100*
  farm census returns, 75
  farm life, 83
  farm owners, 79
  farm workers, 81–2
  farmers, 79–80

farmers' relatives, 80–81
finding and using, 78
information scope, 79–84
maps, 70, 71–4, *72*, *74*, *76*
other records, 85–6
places covered, 70
primary farm records, 75
purpose, 69–70
records, 70–78
scope of information, 11–12
series lists, 73–4
textual records, 74–8, *77*, *81*, *82*, *84*, 107
wider community, 83–4
National Library of Wales, 18
naval operations, 7
NFS *see* National Farm Survey
Northern Ireland, 18
Northumberland, Ordnance Survey key
  sheets, 87

occupations
  National Farm Survey, 80
  tithe surveys, 30
  Valuation Office survey, 59–60
  see also working conditions
occupiers
  National Farm Survey, 79
  tithe surveys, 25, 30
  Valuation Office survey, 59
Office of Works, 4, 7
Orders for Apportionment, 27, 28
Ordnance Office
  estate plans, 5
  military maps, 7
Ordnance Survey maps, 5–6
  County Series, 46–50
  graphic indexes, 89, 92
  large-scale town plans, 51–3
  National Farm Survey, 71
  sheet numbers, 87–92
  Valuation Office survey, 40–41, 46–50, 51–3
overseas maps, 7–9
owners
  National Farm Survey, 79
  tithes, 29
  Valuation Office survey, 59

Palatinate of Chester, 4, 5
Palatinate of Durham, 4, 5
parish boundaries
  Ordnance Survey maps, 6
  tithe surveys, 32, 34
Parish Lists, 85
Parish Summaries of Agricultural Returns, 86
parishes, National Farm Survey, 78, 85
parishioners, tithe surveys, 30
parliamentary boundaries, 6

part-time farmers, 80
payments in kind, tithes, 13–14
'personal failings', National Farm Survey,
    79–80
pests, National Farm Survey, 84
petitions, Valuation Office survey, 67
Pinhoe, Exeter, reformatory school, *82*
plats, 7, 9
plot numbers, tithe apportionments, 26
ploughing-up campaign, 69
primary farm records, 75
PROCAT
    search strategies, 3
    tithe map references, 22, 23
    Valuation Office map references, 54
property sales, 60
protectorates, 7
public schools tithe ownership, 29

railways, 26
record maps, Valuation Office survey, 38,
    40–55, *56*
    arrangement, 43–53
    finding and using, 53–5
    Ordnance Survey County Series, 46–50
    Ordnance Survey large-scale town plans,
        51–3
    record sheet plans, 40, 43
    scale, 41, 51
    valuation districts, 38, 44–5
    what they show, 40–43
rectors, 29
redemption annuities, 15
redemption of tithe rentcharge, 27
Registrar General records, 6
religious dissent, 13
rents, Valuation Office survey, 59
Rhymney Railway Company Form 4-Land, 66
rights of way
    enclosure award maps, 4
    public rights of way, 11, 63
    tithe surveys, 35
roads
    tithe surveys, 32, 34–5
    Valuation Office survey, 60–61
Rose family, Darlaston case study, 101–3

Sackville-West, Vita, 79
Sandringham, Norfolk, *84*
sanitary arrangements, 60
scale
    National Farm Survey, 71
    tithe maps, 19
    Valuation Office survey record maps, 41, 51
schools
    National Farm Survey, *82*
    Valuation Office survey, 62

Scotland
    farm survey, 86
    teinds, 18
    Valuation Office survey, 67
Second World War, 7, 11
second-class tithe maps, 20–21
secular tithe owners, 29
Sissinghurst Castle, 79
site value, 58
social change, 11–12
social status, 30
Spalding, Lincolnshire, *74*
Staffordshire, 101–9
Standidge and Company, 19
statistical analysis, National Farm Survey, 85,
    86
street names, 61
Suffolk, MAF 73 series list, 73, 74
surveyors, tithes, 30–31
Sussex, MAF 73 series list, 73, 74

Teind Court and Commissioners, records, 18
teinds, 18
tenancy
    National Farm Survey, 75
    tithe surveys, 30
    Valuation Office survey, 59
test cases, Valuation Office survey petitions, 67
textual records (MAF 32), National Farm
    Survey, 74–8
    Darlaston case study, 107
Tithe Commutation Act 1837, 18
Tithe Act, 1936, 15
tithe agreements, 15
Tithe Applotment Books, 18
tithe apportionments (IR 29), *21*, 25–8, *29*
    alphabetical arrangement, 16
    altered, 15, 26–8, *95*, *96*
    annotations, 26, 27
    copies, 17–18
    creation, 15
    Darlaston case study, 101, 102, 103, *108–9*
    document references, 17, 25
    Down St Mary case study, 93–4, *93*, *94*
    finding and using, 25–6
    format and contents, 25
    plot numbers, 26
    viewing, 26
tithe areas, 16
tithe awards, 15
tithe barns, *14*, 32
tithe collectors, 31
tithe commissioners, 15
Tithe Commutation Act, 1836, 14
tithe districts
    County Diagrams (Key Sheets), 23
    search strategies, 16–17

tithe files, 28
tithe files (IR 18), 17, 28
    Darlaston case study, 101
    Down St Mary case study, 94
tithe maps (IR 30), 18–25, *24*, *33*
    alphabetical arrangement, 16
    copies, 17–18
    Darlaston case study, 103, *108–9*
    Dawson's recommendations, 18
    details covered, 21–2
    document references, 17, 22–3
    finding and using, 22–4
    first-class maps, 19–20
    second-class maps, 20–21
    styles and scales, 18–19
    viewing, 23–4
tithe maps supplementary (IR 77), 24–5
tithe officials, 30–31
tithe owners, 29
tithe plots, 33
Tithe Redemption Commission, 22, *108*
tithe rentcharge, 14, 15, 25, 59–60
tithe surveys
    Darlaston case study, 101–2, 103, *108–9*
    dates of survey, 15
    Down St Mary case study, 93–4, *93*, *94*, *96*
    information contained, 11, 28–35
    methods, 15
    National Archive records, 16–28
    purpose, 13–14
    search strategies, 16–18
tithe valuation appeals, 94, 95, *95*
tithes in kind, 13–14
tithing, 13
total value, Valuation Office survey, 58
town plans, 6–7, 51–3
trench maps, 7
Tyneside, 89

urbanization, 11, 22, 26
use of maps, 1–2

Valuation Books (Domesday Books), 38, 64
valuation districts, 38, 44–5
valuation divisions, 38
Valuation Office of the Board of Inland
    Revenue, 38
Valuation Office survey, 36–68

Darlaston case study, 102–7, *104–7*
Down St Mary case study, 95, 97–8, *98*
field books, 38, *39*, 55–8, *59*, *62*, *63*
Form 4-Land, 66
Form 36-Land, 66
Form 37-Land, 66
hereditaments, 38, 42, 58, 64
income tax parishes, 38, 42–3, 55, 57, 64
increment value duty, 36–7, 58, 67
information scope, 58–64
map references search, 87–92
methods, 38
miscellaneous records, 66–7
purpose, 36–7
record maps, *37*, 40–55, *41*, 56, *56*
record sheet plans, 40, 43
records not surviving, 57
scope of information, 11
Scotland, 67
search strategies, 40
Valuation Books, 38, 64
working plans, 40, 65–6, *65*
valuers, tithe surveys, 30–31
vicars, 29
voluntary redemption of tithe redemption
    annuity, 27

Wales, 20–21
War diaries, 7
War Office, 2, 5, 6
Warwickshire, National Farm Survey, 78
West Indian Encumbered Estates Commission,
    8, 9
Whitstable, Kent, 61
women
    National Farm Survey, 80
    tithe surveys, 30
Woodhall, Northumberland, estate plan, *5*
woodland, 33
working conditions
    National Farm Survey, 83
    Valuation Office survey, 61
working plans, Valuation Office survey, 40,
    65–6
Worthy Park sugar plantation, Jamaica, *8*

Yorkshire, MAF 73 series list, 73, 74